Building News Literacy

BUILDING NEWS LITERACY

Lessons for Teaching Critical Thinking Skills in Elementary and Middle Schools

Tom Bober

LIBRARIES UNLIMITED®

An Imprint of ABC-CLIO, LLC

Santa Barbara, California • Denver, Colorado

Library of Congress Cataloging in Publication Control Number: 2020043516

ISBN: 978-1-4408-7515-1 (print)
      978-1-4408-7516-8 (ebook)

25 24 23 22 21   1 2 3 4 5

This book is also available as an eBook.

Libraries Unlimited
An Imprint of ABC-CLIO, LLC

ABC-CLIO, LLC
147 Castilian Drive
Santa Barbara, California 93117
www.abc-clio.com

This book is printed on acid-free paper ∞

Manufactured in the United States of America

To my daughters, Emily and Jessica, who have listened
to more news with me than anyone.

Contents

Acknowledgments

The world of news has changed so much over the past several years, and I feel like I have changed over the many months that elapsed as I worked to write this book. It gave me the opportunity to articulate my thoughts about the importance of news literacy for upper elementary and middle school students in ways that I have not previously had the opportunity to do. For that, I am grateful and have people I must thank.

First, thank you to my upper elementary teachers who bring me into conversations with them and their students about information literacy and news literacy. The talks years ago about corroboration, reliability, and credibility certainly revealed the need for these literacies to be addressed and sent me down this path.

Thank you also to David Paige and Jane Cullina at *School Library Connection* who brought me on for two years as the Curriculum Connections Editor. That opportunity pushed me to grow as a school librarian and develop the ideas that were emerging in my own library. The inspiration for this book comes from a monthly post written during that time, and I couldn't be more grateful for the encouragement and good fortune to have worked with you.

The biggest thank-you goes to Sharon Coatney, my editor for this book. After working with me on my first title, she thought I had another book in me. After a healthy conversation and some time to reflect, I agreed. Having someone believe you can do something before even you do is a wonderful feeling.

Speaking of having people believe in me, I must finally thank my family: my daughters, who regularly listen to me talk through opportunities and options; and my wife, Jen, who agrees to share her own expertise and perspective by reading every word I write. I could not do these things without your support and belief in me.

1

News Literacy in Elementary and Middle Schools?

Recently, I walked the playground during an upper elementary recess and eavesdropped on conversations. I wondered if I could hear evidence of my students being aware of what was going on in the news. It didn't take me long to find that evidence: it was all over the playground.

One student was talking about some recent flooding that had happened locally and, in a jealous tone, noted that some students got to stay home a day because a school district had made the decision to call off school for student safety. Another student was joking about a political figure with a surprising amount of detail, which revealed to me that he had information that had only recently been reported. A third student was proudly sharing information about her favorite movie series. She knew more than what would be found in a commercial. Her part of the conversation with friends contained box office information and announcements about upcoming movies in the series.

Later, I approached these three students and asked them where they had heard the news that they shared. The anecdotal results showed that all their information came from different places. Upon asking more widely, though, patterns appeared. These upper elementary students were getting news information by viewing or listening to news with a parent or other trusted adult, hearing news shared with them by a trusted adult or peer, or seeking out news on topics that interested them using personal or family devices.

Next, I visited our middle school lunchroom to see how sixth- and seventh-grade students' news experiences compared. I was surprised to find the number of students who had ready information about news of the day.

More than one shared news about an earthquake that had happened the day before in another country. Several shared current political stories. A recent school shooting was concerning to another table of students that I spoke with.

It appeared that there were similarities in awareness of news between these two groups, but as I dug deeper, differences also appeared. Several middle school students shared that they learned about news by receiving notifications on their phones. Asked if they read these news reports, most shared that they did not read further than the headline and maybe a few lines of the article. Others saw news on social media apps, despite being below the required age to have an account. One student, when asked about news, shared his love of conspiracy theories and the YouTuber he often watched.

We live in a world where our upper elementary and middle school students are more aware than ever of what is going on around them. Gone are the days when young children's view of the world would be shaped primarily by what they overheard between adults at the dinner table. Sure, the adults are still talking, and the children are still listening, but now there are so many more places to hear about the news events of the day.

Many of those places do not include the adults in children's lives, and because of that, we cannot be there to help them interpret all of the news they hear. Instead, we need to give them a skill set that encourages them to identify, interpret, and evaluate the news they hear and connect it to their own lives.

That is a tall order. These are things that not all adults are adept at doing. So why not wait until later in middle school or even high school? Why not wait until they are older and more mature? The truth is that we should not wait. If our children and students are taking in news on a regular (even daily) basis, we should be giving them the tools to deal with that information.

Our upper elementary and middle school students are in a transition phase as to how they receive information and news. At some point—and it is different for every child—many go from their parents or other adults in their lives being in control of the news they hear to news being shared with them by social media, apps, or peers. This transition makes it a critical time to instill a set of skills that will allow children to be sophisticated consumers of news and information, both at this moment in their lives and moving forward. *This is the time to teach news literacy.*

WHERE DO ELEMENTARY AND MIDDLE SCHOOL STUDENTS GET THEIR NEWS?

Between YouTube, podcasts, news websites, news being shared on social media, news apps, and pop-up notifications on phones and devices, elementary and middle school children with their own devices have many more opportunities to hear news, and to hear opinions about that news, than was available in the past.

They also are exposed to those news sources that adults in their lives put in front of them. Parents may have news on in the home or car radio that students passively hear. Teachers may subscribe to *Time for Kids* or online news services like Newsela. School or public librarians can house subscriptions to *Sports Illustrated Kids* or other topical periodicals that share timely news targeted to younger readers.

This, like my walking through my elementary school playground and middle school lunchroom, is all anecdotal, though. What do studies show about tweens and their interactions with the news?

One report that may be the most telling is a 2017 report from Common Sense Media titled *News and America's Kids: How Young People Perceive and Are Impacted by the News* (Robb, 2017). Roughly one-third of the youth surveyed are between the ages of ten and twelve and in some of the data, they are specifically identified as "tweens."

The report shows some current realities as well as trends as children transition from tweens to teens. First, tweens do get their news from a variety of sources, including parents, friends, television, social media, and apps, among other places. Looking at tweens and teens, there is a noticeable transition in where they get their news. Similar to what I found in my school recess and lunch walks, as children get older they increasingly get news from online sources, while still getting news from adults in their lives. This trend might be explained by another element of the survey: an acknowledgment of getting news from adults but a preference for getting it from social media.

This adds an important element to how educators think about teaching news literacy. It is unlikely that upper elementary and middle school students will be learning about news literacy on Snapchat or TikTok while in their classroom or library. Teachers and librarians can't cover every format or new app that is used by students or may be the next hot app to come along in the future. What we can do is be aware that how we (adults) access news is likely not how our students do or will access it.

Part of that awareness comes from not only talking with our students about where they learn about their news, but also honoring the news and news access points that they value and share with us as educators. When students share with me that they receive all of their news on Snapchat, then I am undervaluing what they share with me if I immediately point them toward other news access points. This does not mean I cannot expose them to other news access points, such as websites or even other social media platforms. I should, however, consider when I decide to share that information and not do it at the expense of building a relationship as a news literacy mentor with students.

I also am deliberate about giving value to certain types of news over others. I have spoken with students who value up-to-date news about movies, new book releases, or a new clothing line or brand of shoes being released beyond all else. To build skills, this book does not rely on those interests, which fall outside of the typical school curriculum, but it also does not dismiss them. News literacy is not dependent on a specific topic or type of news. I want to help my students develop news literacy that will allow them to navigate *any* type of news. That is done by giving them experiences to build news literacy and also helping them connect those skills to the news topics and access points in the rest of their lives.

We don't need unique news literacy skills to speak to every possible access point or news topic, but we do need to be sure that we are addressing how our students access news and that the news literacy skills we are introducing aren't in conflict with the access points and topics that they encounter in their lives outside of the school day. Such conflict can be exacerbated when educators ignore or even dismiss how students access news outside of school or the topics they value.

How news is perceived is also an element of the Common Sense Media study and is equally revealing. When asked what sources they trust news from, tweens overwhelmingly select family. This may not be surprising, but what may be surprising is that only about a quarter of those same elementary and middle school students trust the information they see, hear, or read from news organizations. This may be partially explained by how the public defines *news*. I'll discuss that in the next part of this chapter.

When we look at where upper elementary and middle school students get their news, one source that plays a larger role the older they get is their peers. Whether news is shared in the lunchroom, the playground, or through social media, this last statistic should cause concern. In that same Common Sense Media study, almost 60% of all youth surveyed said they had or were unsure if they had shared a story that was inaccurate.

This lack of certainty about the accuracy of news is a sign of our times. This book does not delve deeply into "fake news," information that presents itself as news but instead is intentional disinformation. What it does instead is try to give students skills that they can utilize in regard to everything they perceive to be news. Some of the information students are encountering will likely turn out not to be news. It may be other types of information such as advertising. It may be disinformation intentionally represented as news. All of those things are important to identify. Lessons within this book will help students do just that: look at information intentionally to determine its purpose and intended audience.

Equally important is for students to be able to interact with true news. When encountering news we should all work to understand, connect, communicate, and question the information within the material we are reading, watching, or listening. If students are truly news literate and are doing all of these things, they will not only deeply interact with news. They will also be much more likely to be able to identify inaccurate information and "fake news." There certainly is value in books and lessons that focus on inaccurate and fake news, but if those experiences are not built upon a strong foundation of news literacy, we may be doing a disservice to our students.

DEFINING NEWS

I like simple definitions, especially when I am going to share those definitions with students. There are lessons later in the book that do just that with definitions for *news, facts, opinions,* and other terms novice news consumers should be familiar with. Before those lessons, though, it may be beneficial for teachers to develop their own definitions of *news*. Those definitions will determine how teachers see news, what news is brought to students, and how news is addressed in the classroom. For the purposes of this book, I use the following definition: *News is a broadcast or published report to inform about recent events.*

The immediacy of the event being reported differentiates news from other information they hear during the day from their teachers, textbooks, and online databases. The fact that it is broadcast or published begins to limit what information we describe as news based or where that information comes from. This definition of news determines what is selected when searching for news or when categorizing information as news.

It would be wrong to assume that every upper elementary and middle school student has a definition for *news*. It is more likely that they have examples. Part of this may be due to news not arriving in a single format, but we should focus on the timing of information being shared as well as how it is delivered. There are likely examples of news reporting that students have not encountered yet. Without that working definition to guide their determination and evaluation of what is in front of them, students will likely not identify these different examples as news. The lack of a definition may also be a foundational reason why students are concerned about the accuracy of the information they are sharing.

Once students have a definition of news, nonexamples can be helpful in clarifying that definition. Many news aggregators contain information or stories that would not, under my definition, be considered news. Typically, the stories I see that fall into this nonexample category are interest stories that fall outside of what can be described as recent events. One example is a story about nostalgic elements from a past decade. Even though it is a published report, this type of story does not meet the requirement of being about a recent event. Therefore, it wouldn't be described as news even though it may be gathered or included with news stories in a news-aggregating app or website.

Another nonexample of news is published material that is focused on recent events but is not a report but instead a commentary. Many televised shows on major news networks are foundationally based on commentary. The news that is offered is shared within the context of commenting on it, but the commentary is what drives the programming. These can be confusing examples. Looking at the published program over time may provide insight.

A final nonexample is information that is current and even shared over social networks but not published or broadcast. If I post a photo on social media of a water main break near my school, one might wonder if that is "publishing." I would argue that it is not. These types of brief accounts, photos, or videos from events in the moment are more appropriately categorized as *primary sources* of an event. In published or broadcast news, news consumers often see these as embedded or referenced elements within a news report, but these elements themselves are not news. Can students, then, publish news? They certainly do through school or classroom newspapers or broadcasts. Those are specific efforts to collect current information, synthesize that information, and share it with a defined group. This can be viewed as similar to what a professional news organization does in its reporting. Also like those professional organizations, student organizations that publish or broadcast news do it more than once, often at regular intervals. This is another major difference between this student sharing of news compared to sharing other types of current information over social media.

This foundational definition of news, along with nonexamples, can be built upon to explore other layers of how elementary and middle school students describe and define news. The possibilities for organizing news in an effort to describe it are limitless. A class's or student's collection of news at the moment may help guide the decisions of how news can be organized. The following examples are a few major categories that may assist in guiding thinking.

By Format

As we look to define *news,* one way is to determine how it is received. I've already mentioned several formats through which people can view, listen to, or read news, including television, YouTube, radio, apps, and social media.

While the idea of how news is acquired may not be an immediate way to define news itself, it certainly should be taken into consideration as we craft our definitions. Where our students find news may make it more or less likely for them to interact with that news in meaningful ways. My middle school students who rarely read beyond the headline come to mind. Although their experiences are not dissimilar from some news that I receive daily over my phone, knowing when, why, and how we interact with some news and not other news is worth considering.

One thing to try to avoid is always sharing news from one format alone. It is important for students to see news in a variety of formats even if some of those formats are not ones we would typically utilize in the classroom. Arguments can be made that it is unnecessary to bring the print newspaper back into the classroom, but some students do respond well to print news. There are regular publications that classroom and schools can subscribe to. Although much news that students encounter will be accessed digitally, students having the experience of interacting with text, audio, and video news in that digital format can broaden their experience with interacting with and identifying news outside of the school day.

Educators shouldn't ignore any of these news formats. We may not always be able to interact with them fully in the classroom or library, but there certainly are opportunities to illustrate how we can demonstrate good news literacy skills in every news format we present to students.

By Geography

Another way to view news is by seeing where the news itself is focused. Steven Waldman, former senior advisor to the chair of the FCC, explored this perspective as part of a 2011 report. Waldman looks at different geographic focal levels for news from the hyperlocal to international news. Think of hyperlocal as neighborhood news. Other levels of news are geographically focused at the city, state, national, and international levels.

When thinking about different stories that fit these geographic focal points, the previous indicator of format can be brought into play. When there is neighborhood news, where would a student hear about it? Likely not on

YouTube, and possibly not the radio. Though the answer certainly will differ for individual students, trends could emerge as educators discuss news literacy with them.

How do students hear about the park being remodeled down the street? What were they listening to when they saw the news about the new sports team coming to the major city in their state? Where were they when they heard about the latest national weather emergency? How did they come across that international human interest story?

Another reason a geographic filter on news may be worth considering is that students may be drawn to a certain geographic level of news. Some students may find those stories closest to home to be most impactful. Other students may find the national headlines more interesting because it gives them a view beyond their own backyard. For educational purposes, though, bringing in news stories from multiple geographic viewpoints when working toward students' news literacy is advisable.

One area of news not mentioned in Waldman's report that may pertain to students at the elementary or middle school level is school news that is published or broadcast by other students. From a geographic perspective, this news would likely report on events and individuals very close to the students' lives and therefore be of high interest to many students. Although the lessons within this book do not expand into this area of student-created news, the ideas therein would also come into play if students are taking on the role of news organization through a class or club at school.

This option of school-based news may be more available than you realize. In my school we have one fifth-grade teacher whose students publish several issues of a newspaper every year. For her students, it is an ongoing collaborative writing activity. News stories are often about new staff members, newly released books, or other stories of high interest for the class. That same publication easily becomes a chance for other students in the school, as news consumers, to interact with local news and practice news literacy skills.

Hard News and Soft News

There is also the split of hard news and soft news. *Hard news* can be defined as breaking and up-to-the-minute news. It may find a natural home in the classroom when focusing on a service learning project, making a real-world connection between science curriculum and a new scientific discovery, or when news is talked about in the classroom for social-emotional support.

Soft news is often more fun and, for some students, of greater interest. News about sports teams, celebrities, shows and movies, and new books all fall under this category, which can entertain as well as inform about current events.

Hard news often seems like a natural fit for teachers to incorporate into student learning. In some ways it may feel more important or substantial. On a grander scale that may be true. Certainly, if there is a curriculum connection, hard news can be an important resource. We have a grade level of students who write persuasive essays as part of their language arts curriculum.

Because of the framing of the project, students often choose perspectives from a larger topic for their research. Issues around climate change, personal rights, or child welfare can be common large topics that students dive into to select a more narrowly focused area. News stories that can be described as hard news are often used in multiple ways. The stories help students broaden their understanding of a topic so they can focus their attention on an element of the larger issue for their writing. Those news stories also serve as factual support for the persuasive claims they make in their writing. Without this type of news, this particular writing project may not be possible. The students' work certainly wouldn't have the quality that it does without it.

It may not seem that soft news has a place in the classroom, but it certainly has a place in many students' lives. Bringing news stories of new literature from favorite authors into a reading lesson or connecting a news report related to a television show, movie, or sporting event that a student watched to journaling the student has done can bring news literacy into a daily class meeting or a student's school life.

Another important area where soft news can play a large role in the classroom is in building relationships. This important aspect of classroom management, especially at the beginning of the school year, could easily incorporate soft news. These types of news stories are often of high interest to students. As students share areas of interest to them, soft news events are bound to be brought into the conversation. Teachers can search for a news report related to the event so that the student can share it with the whole class. Though this may not be the time for deep news literacy lessons, it can give students experience being news consumers and, if done at the beginning of the year, can give the teacher an opportunity to formatively assess students as news consumers in an informal environment while giving all students a set of shared experiences to draw from later when interacting with other news. Educators' bringing soft news into the classroom based on student interest also gives opportunities for light modeling as they search and interact with the news stories.

By Creator or Reporter

Most students take in news from a variety of sources, but there are likely a few that are preferred. I spoke with one middle school student who often watched the reports of a national anchor because that anchor had visited his sister's high school. Another student received much of her superhero movie news from a particular website. A friend often watched a specific YouTube channel for the same movie information before they talked about upcoming films.

Some students may not initially have preferred sources for news, especially if they do not seek out news as news consumers. Those same students may not even consider where the news they interact with comes from until it is pointed out through a news literacy lesson. Throughout the year, look for opportunities to point out news creators and reporters who repeatedly have news in the classroom or library conversation. Invite students to share favorite news sources.

These differences between students can be a focus of discussion as students begin to articulate their preferences for specific news sources. Why choose one news source over another? What is it about a news reporter that makes this person appealing? Even though the news items themselves may not connect to content curriculum, students' trusted sources for news are often real-world examples of reliable sources. These are not only key in developing news literacy, they can also help students understand issues of reliable sources and credible information when it comes to information literacy.

There may be times when we organize how we view the news we receive by where we receive it. Of course, this may layer into another organizational element. For example, students may go to certain sources for hard news and very different sources for soft news. The preference for a specific news source may have just as much to do with the format in which the source delivers the reporting as any other factor. In other cases, the topic may also be a central driver that narrows down the possible news sources that a student may prefer.

By Legitimacy

I will not spend much time in this book writing about the term "fake news." Disinformation in reported information news certainly is a reason to teach news literacy skills to students. This is likely the most undesirable type of "news" because it is not truly news at all.

Other elements within news may cause the viewer to view it as less legitimate than other news. An overabundance of commentary and bias included in news, or the intentional nonreporting on information to elevate other reported information, can cause viewers to question the legitimacy of the news itself.

I often talk with students about upcoming technology. New phones, watches, and technology accessories are typically released on a predictable timeline and with each pending release comes news of rumored upcoming features. Through our conversations, we have certainly talked about news reports about technology products and features that did not come to fruition. On a favorite site of mine, after new products are announced, they give what they describe as a "rumor roundup." The site revisits predictions and the news sources that reported them. Through the experience, sources emerge that are more and less reliable. Over time, the reliability of the sources is usually confirmed through multiple rounds of reporting. If there is a wide enough number of sources on a topic of student interest, students can also compare reporting across sources. If reports are varied, students can begin to think about the legitimacy of sources as a way to further categorize the news.

The reliability or trustworthiness of a source and the credibility or believability of the information is at the core of determining the legitimacy of news. Those determinations can shift as students learn more information about the topic being reported on. This topic is specifically explored in lessons later in the book.

RECRUITING EVERYONE IN THE EFFORT

Looking at how news is received doesn't help us answer a question that may be lingering with you and certainly lingers with me. Why, in the Common Sense Media study, did only 25% of respondents trust news from news organizations? Where is the breakdown? There are many possibilities. There are so many that I believe it is beyond the scope of one educator to address news literacy within the confines of a year. Not only is that an impossible task given other curricular expectations, but how students access news and react to it changes as they mature and their lives inside and outside of school change. Finally, the medium of how news is delivered continues to change.

Building news literacy can be an effort in which everyone takes part. There is room at the table for more than the classroom teacher. The library media specialist brings a strong background in how to process and react to information. School reading teachers and reading specialists have a deep understanding of students' processing of text as well as how students can react to what they read. Instructional technology specialists have an ever-evolving knowledge of the latest technologies and how those tools are used to share information. Even if they are not up on the latest social media app, they may be the adults best suited to gather information on it, understand how students are using it, and compare it to other applications with which the rest of the adults at the table may be more familiar. Administrators and coaches, though possibly not having an ongoing interest in news literacy, can help make connections among elementary and middle school classroom teachers, librarians, other educators, and curriculum.

Parents and students need a seat at this table, too. Although neither will be implementing formal lessons during the school day, each plays an important role in the forming of those lessons and the learning that takes place. Students sharing their reality when it comes to news they read, see, and listen to outside of the classroom or library walls gives a perspective by which lessons in news literacy can be customized. When parents know what learning is taking place, they can reinforce those skills when they and their children encounter news outside of the school day and environment.

Teaching news literacy is also a long-term effort. Implementing a strong news literacy program that focuses on upper elementary and middle school students does not imply that these skills will not have to be revisited as students leave middle school and enter high school. These skills should be returned to as students are confronted with different types of news and interact with it in different ways.

An ongoing effort that encompasses educators from different specialties and even different buildings, as well as students and parents, requires two things to succeed: communication and transparency. Varied communications can be brought to the table. Formal meetings, water-cooler conversations, planning sessions, and information gathering can all take place to accomplish goals around news literacy. Those goals can be varied as well. Understanding current teaching strategies and environments, explaining student's current news interactions, being exposed to news delivery methods, and exploring vertical teaching possibilities are all topics that can be included in large and small conversations. Matching up the best type of communication with the goal at the moment can result in purposeful planning that benefits students and informs everyone.

Without transparency, that communication will be for naught. Educators and teachers should be encouraged to be transparent about what they do not know. Gaps could be about children's news experiences. They could be in supporting children as they grow in their news literacy. Transparency regarding these gaps can also include asking for help from a colleague or one of the other groups involved in this effort. This transparency must also span across grade levels and buildings. Teachers need to know what students' prior experiences were as they developed news literacy skills. This is especially important for schools and districts where there isn't a specific news literacy curriculum.

An additional point to be made is that with regard to these different goals for individuals to get together, educators take on different roles. Specifically, there are moments or entire meetings where students may drive the meeting agenda. For example, if the goal of a meeting is to gather an understanding of news literacy from the student's perspective, the student should be doing the majority of the speaking and the educator the majority of the listening.

I have been part of roundtables where gathering information from students has been the goal. In these cases, my colleagues and I made sure certain elements were in place:

- Have a diverse group of students to gather as many different voices as possible. Space, time, and other logistics may have to be taken into consideration. It may not be necessary, or make sense, to talk to an entire class or grade level to have a rich opportunity to share, given other limitations.
- Have a limited number of educators as part of the overall group. In our situation, we had one facilitator and one scribe.
- Be deliberate in how participants are chosen. Obviously there are opportunities to bring anyone who is interested to the table, but there are other times when a sampling of voices meets the needs of the moment. Think about those voices that are not heard as often or as loudly.
- Be selective about the adults in the room. We purposely did not use classroom teachers to facilitate or scribe because they could be perceived as "evaluating" students as they must do in the classroom.
- Be clear with students about the purpose of the meeting. We started our meeting by sharing that the students' honest opinions and stories were going to affect decisions that teachers made. They were helping us so that we could do a better job in teaching them.
- Facilitate; do not teach. A set of questions to guide the conversation is appropriate. Asking clarifying or follow-up questions is also appropriate. The facilitator should be aware of her or his tone in addition to what she or he says. If what is said or how it is said does not facilitate gathering the desired information from the students, the educator should either say it differently or not at all.

- Be transparent. We often, unintentionally, had a curious student next to the educator scribing. As the adult scribe typed away, it was not unusual for a student on either side to lean over to see what was being typed. Not only did we tell students that we were only writing down their words as exactly as possible, we invited them to check as their sharings were being recorded.

We felt that approaching student involvement in this way fostered trust and brought students to the table as valued members of the conversation. Of course, this is not the only structure that can be useful when bringing everyone to the table. Similar considerations may be taken when involving parents. Prioritizing student and parent voices at the appropriate time and stepping back from the role of educator while still listening through that lens can meaningfully involve everyone in the process of developing and implementing news literacy in upper elementary and middle school students.

WHAT THIS BOOK ATTEMPTS TO DO

With twenty-four-hour news, podcasts, news websites, news apps, and pop-up notifications on phones and devices, our students have a huge number of opportunities to interact with news and to hear opinions about that news. Whether they are on the playground or their phone, students will have the opportunity to share that news with others.

Chapter 2 addresses the current reality of receiving and sharing news. The challenges that arise from that current news reality are laid out. Among them are distinguishing between people and organizations reporting news and those sharing that reporting, distinguishing between information in news and how we react to it, and emphasizing the importance of reliable sources and credible information. Finally, the chapter briefly looks at traditional approaches to news literacy and why they may not address the current reality.

Chapter 3 takes the entirety of news literacy and breaks it into its many parts. Focusing on news literacy as a whole may seem insurmountable, but hyperfocusing on one literacy that helps to make up the whole of news literacy can be a useful approach. The chapter looks at literacies around text, visuals, graphics, and audiovisuals.

The chapter also makes the case that is the foundation for the lessons within Chapter 4: that there are direct connections to be made between news literacy and historical literacy. Most directly stated, the historical literacy skills that we teach students can be targeted to news stories from historical events and individuals as a way to teach some news literacy skills. Those skills can be built upon with additional and modified skills to address delivery formats of today's news.

Chapter 4 consists of a series of lessons. Pairing the teaching of news literacy and history, parts of each lesson in this book encourage learning through using news from a historic time period. This allows both content skills and news literacy skills to be taught simultaneously. Although the lessons focus on a variety of news topics throughout history, it is expected that educators may want to locate historically based news that is relevant to the content students are learning.

Your school or district may have access to specific news databases. Free databases such as Chronicling America (https://chroniclingamerica.loc.gov) or the American Archive of Public Broadcasting (https://americanarchive.org) can be great resources to access historical news content, and they are available to everyone. They are used extensively as resources for the lessons within this book for that very reason. Local organizations such as museums, public libraries, and academic libraries may have holdings of historical local news sources as well as databases of historical national news sources.

Each lesson also includes ways to adapt the historically based activity using current news. These parts of the lessons describe considerations when incorporating current news sources into the teaching of a specific news literacy skill. Because today's news becomes tomorrow's "old news," I do not offer specific examples of news of the day. Instead, I focus the adaptations on students being exposed to a variety of formats and delivery methods of news and how those affect the focus of the lesson and student learning.

Current news may come from a variety of sources. Students may have access to dual print and online platforms such as *Time for Kids* or online-only platforms such as Newsela to connect with news specifically created for student consumption. Educators should not be limited to those sources, however. Reputable local and national news sources can be used. Social media links can be shared to show students how news is presented in different formats and venues.

It is the role of the educator to curate current news not originally intended for students. If students are interacting with news not originally intended for them, educators should ensure that it is accessed in a way that is safe. That may mean not sharing direct links if the learning does not call for it, but instead sharing screenshots or printouts of the news. Videos can often be viewed through sites that filter out ads and other video suggestions. If students are using links or educators are linking to news as part of the class, the educators should be sure that the links are not blocked by school or district filters as part of the curation process.

Not all lessons work in all environments. Time, resources, and prior learning all come into play. Each lesson also contains suggestions to differentiate the lesson to engage students in different ways, extend the learning, or adapt to different elements of learning.

Each lesson also contains an exit slip. The exit slip is meant to be a formative check on where individual students are regarding skills and thinking connected to news literacy. Many lessons employ pair, group, and whole-class discussions that encourage students to think through their developing news literacy skills and allow educators to gather an overall idea of student understanding. These exit slips give an opportunity for each individual student to reflect. Because these lessons can be used with a range of grade levels, and news literacy skills should be continually evolving through those years, there are no accompanying scoring guides.

Finally, lessons have an organizer to help students organize their thinking throughout the lesson. In many lessons, students are asked to document findings from a news report. If the news article is printed, students and teachers may find annotating directly on the text to be more beneficial and easier than using the organizer. It may also be a choice given to students who have access to both the article and the organizer.

Finally, let me also speak about what this book does *not* intend to do. It is not a comprehensive news literacy program to be implemented in upper elementary and middle school grades. Instead, there are elements throughout these four chapters that can foster discussion and help to build a news literacy curriculum. Other features can be incorporated into an existing curriculum to incorporate news literacy into other learning. As mentioned earlier, the lessons can be used as they stand, but they are not intended to be the only experiences to teach news literacy. In addition to the adaptations that are already incorporated into the lessons, different news topics and formats can be utilized. As students share their reality as news consumers, other learning experiences may present themselves. The lessons within this book can serve as inspiration. Lastly, this book on developing news literacy is not meant to compete with other books on the same or similar topic. Some other books on developing news literacy focus on different ages or different elements of news consumption. Specifically, there are several books that look at identifying and dealing with "fake news" (e.g., Waldman, 2018). As I mention elsewhere, a solid foundation in news literacy is key to identifying and interacting with misinformation and disinformation in the news. Therefore, those books do not compete with this book, but instead complement it in developing the fullest range of skills and experiences as students develop news literacy throughout their school experience.

Using both historical news and tools for students to successfully access historical documents, students can begin to acquire news literacy skills in upper elementary and middle school. Bridging the use of those skills to current news reinforces the skills and gives students immediate practice as they grow into news-literate individuals.

2

Challenges to Be Addressed by Developing News Literacy in Students

If there was only one issue of concern when it came to news literacy, there wouldn't be so much conversation around the topic. Instead, there are multiple reasons why it appears that news literacy is more of a concern, especially in the past few years. Stony Brook University's Center for News Literacy identifies four reasons that are challenges to news literacy:

- The overwhelming amount of information.
- Technology increasing the likelihood of sharing misinformation.
- The speed of information being shared and acquired.
- Seeing only information that confirms our own beliefs.

These concerns are technology focused, but there are fundamental elements in play about how people access news and how they interact with it.

I see two major categories for classifying the challenges of teaching news literacy. First, there are student challenges. Upper elementary and middle school students have more independent access to news. They are learning to maneuver means of getting news and other information in ways that are evolving quickly. The helpful parent or teacher may not be there during times when the novice to news literacy is struggling internally with or confused by the news he or she is encountering. There may be times when that trusted adult is not there to help. Other times, it may mean that children will not ask for that help. Instead, they go it alone or rely on peers who may also be struggling with or confused by the same issues. There can be a solidarity for young learners in the idea that they are struggling through this challenge of navigating news together. Unfortunately, that solidarity does not necessarily result in the development of strong news literacy skills.

There are also educator challenges. Educators must challenge themselves to fully understand and embrace their students' realities. If the ultimate goal is to affect how students interact with news of all types outside of the school day, then understanding how, when, and why they interact with news is the first task. Although it may seem counterproductive to look toward news from the past to address this, finding the bridges between news of the past and today can give students more opportunity to practice newly acquired skills in different situations. This allows students to interact with news in ways that are connected to their current curriculum, allowing for layered instruction during a limited amount of time. It also can highlight that students have solutions within themselves for understanding and making meaning from the news that do not directly involve the screen on which they read or view that news.

The following considerations are a combination of these student and educator challenges. Some may be viewed as solely student or solely educator challenges. Others may be seen as challenges for both groups. It is not my intention to exclude parents from the discussion of these challenges. Parents will, at various times, sit side-by-side with students as they learn about strategies to build news literacy, and at other times will sit side-by-side with educators as they learn about their child's reality as a news consumer and help the child navigate newly learned strategies to develop news literacy skills. As parents share their own reality as news consumers and news messengers to their students, their role in meeting the challenges to building news literacy will become apparent.

READING DIGITAL VS. PRINT

How often do students pick up newspapers or even magazines? If you are not sure, ask your students—but I would venture a guess that it rarely happens. Instead, the students whom I have spoken with are more likely to hear news from a parent or the radio or read it on a device.

Focusing on the news that is read, many educators realize that reading digital news is different from reading print news. The type of device students read from may affect exactly what they see, but they are likely to come across in-story links, advertisements, related content, and reader comments. All of this can distract from the news that they intended to read.

This is not a reason to keep students from online news. It is, instead, a step in attempting to understand the reality of news that students encounter. Understanding the presence of these online distractions also opens educators to invite students to talk about the reality of their news consumption. What do students do when an advertisement pops up in the middle of their YouTube video? How many have inadvertently clicked on a strategically placed advertisement as they were trying to scroll through a news story? Did they realize what had happened? What did they do next? Not all students will have the same experience with reading, listening to, and viewing news online. Giving them the opportunity to share those experiences may not only inform the educator but also share some best practices and reveal gaps in experiences. These findings can focus a teacher's discussion and news encounters with students. This focus can result in a targeted news literacy message that students can take and immediately implement as news consumers.

When it comes to research, many teachers and standards emphasize the importance of students using both print and digital resources. I think the same can be said for news. Reading print news, even if it is simply a news story printed off from a website, can give students practice in discrete news literacy skills. They can use these experiences with print news to identify fact and opinion within a news story, identify perspective, or practice asking questions based on the news story. Experiences with print news allow students to focus their attention on these skills instead of the multitasking of news literacy and information literacy skills that they often must balance when reading, watching, or listening to news online.

Our instruction of news literacy skills should not stop there, though. Students need to be exposed to the news online. Some of that can be accomplished through trusted news sites that are tailored for student use. Other experiences should be on news sites that are used by the general public.

Educators should not do this with fear, but with planning. Too much caution can make me feel as if I'm doing something dangerous, something I should not be doing. Instead, I want to be overly informed about what experience my students will have. Teachers should heavily browse news stories that they plan to share with students. Putting themselves in the students' shoes, educators should click on links and look for likely distractions. Educators can also look for advantages of online news as compared to print. Identifying links that extend the news story, noting additions to the story as the news evolves, and recognizing other changing and interactive features of online news can show an educator the depth that an online story holds for student learning. Depending on their prior experiences with online news, teachers may decide to be simply aware of these advantages without initially promoting them to students. Allowing students to find and promote these features to classmates can enable more authentic learning experiences and empower students in their evolution as they become more news literate. As educators become more adept at incorporating features of online news into lessons and giving time for students to take advantage of them, the structures of lessons may change to accommodate the different environments where students are reading news.

This open type of exploration in some online news sites may be too unstructured for some students. As students begin to get acclimated to reading news in an online environment, educators may also model browsing through a digital news story. Distractions such as advertisements or comments should not be ignored, but pointed out to make students more aware of what sits alongside a digital news story but is not part of that story. Similarly, embedded links within the article to related news stories should also be highlighted, clicked on, and explored as part of fully comprehending a news topic. As teachers work with students in this way, they may also consider transitioning from modeler to navigator. When students share their own observations about online news resources, the teacher can navigate based on what students want to explore. This can allow a natural transition into students independently exploring online news in their learning.

Though a step further distanced from viewing news online, teachers can also share screenshots of news stories. Distractions can still be pointed to. Links embedded in the article can be captured as well for a richer experience. This can provide a more controlled experience for students who are just beginning to explore digital news. This type of exploration may be useful when beginning to use online news or an online news site. Screenshots capture a moment of a site that may regularly change with updated news stories. The static screenshot can also become an assured resource for an educator to use when wanting to introduce elements such as navigation features or likely distractions.

I would be remiss if I did not address news video and audio when referencing digital news. Often the audiovisual is paired with the written story online. The viewer chooses whether to watch or listen to the story, to read it, or to engage in some combination of both. This addition to the digital news story can add a layer of comprehension and engagement for students. Word pronunciation, emphasis within sentences, and additional visuals can provide more context for students watching or listening to a digital story. Closed captioning on most news videos brings a reading element into the experience. This can help with comprehension by providing an additional layer of media for students. There can be drawbacks as well. Many embedded videos within a news story will automatically play advertisements or progress to another video. All of these occurrences can be explored in a guided environment so they do not cause confusion to the students viewing them.

TRUSTING THE MESSENGER AND THE MESSAGE

Students need to acquire the skill of questioning not only the message within news, but also the messenger who shares the news. Educators may give students opportunities to question the news itself. Students should have lessons in which they are asked to wrestle with whether the information they receive from a news story is believable. They may also have the chance to look at the individual, website, or organization that is delivering the news and determine if those sources are trustworthy. But how often are students asked to step back and question how that news was actually received? Who was the messenger, and how does that affect the news message that they received?

Often students do not question the messenger because we as educators *are* the messengers. We are delivering the news to our students, whether it is the student-friendly news pamphlet delivered each month or the online article we share with them via a link in our digital classroom. We fulfill this role, and there is no reason to question us because most of our students consider us to be trusted messengers. The same can be said of our students' parents as news messengers. We all have curated the news that is being delivered to these students.

The way that students receive news is changing, though, and in today's digital age the newer messengers may not have earned that same level of trust. Students who have a presence in online social networks will experience this to the greatest degree. Sharing news of all types as well as commentary about the news is possible in all online social networks and people of all ages will see the news that is shared by friends, family, acquaintances, and connections. What we want our news-literate students to do is see not only the news but also the news messenger.

I have had conversations with parents about checking their child's online social media connections. I, as a parent, have played that role myself. What I have found is that parents and children are comfortable with different online social circles. Some children may only be in contact with immediate family. Others are, at a young age, in contact with family, friends from school, members of teams, people they met at a summer camp, and maybe even friends of friends. I make no judgment on where those limits are drawn, nor do I even make recommendations. There are others who have expertise to speak to those issues.

My point is simply that when it comes to sharing current and breaking information in social networks, not everyone does it equally well or does it in the same way. As students begin their journey on social media, they should know exactly that. Understanding that others within their online social circles make mistakes in what they share can cause students to have a healthy skepticism when they see news that is shared online. Before they even ask themselves what the news story is about or whether the source of the news is reliable, they should consider the news messenger. What does the student know about that person, not as a friend, relative, or acquaintance, but as a person who shares news? If that is a question students ask from the onset, it can be very telling and useful. While this question can help expose potentially false or misleading news, it also potentially tells a lot about a news story. Consider that others often share news from a limited number of sources, about a limited number of topics, and from a limited number of perspectives. If students have an idea of what those sources, topics, and perspectives are with specific news messengers, that knowledge can help them approach the news that has been shared. Knowing the news-sharing traits of a news messenger may help students know what the story is likely about, decide if they are going to click on the story, and even whether they may view it more critically. What an advantage! Knowing news messengers and considering them as a part of how they access news can help students in their own journey of becoming more news literate.

The recognition of news messengers, as well as the situation of having news messengers online in social media platforms, will be in flux with students in upper elementary and middle school. As they enter this stage of their schooling, they likely already have mostly trusted sources for their news. Parents, teachers, librarians, and other trusted adults share the news with children. These adults also often do more than that. They may scaffold to help students understand the news. They can be a model for how news is processed and integrated into one's life. Teachers and parents can continue to play that role with news found by their students and children online. Discussions led by students and children, focused on what they have seen, read, or heard in news they've encountered online, can open opportunities for adults. Teachers and parents can take these chances to model behavior in how they react to the news. When those are taken as modeling opportunities and not teaching or judging opportunities, children may be more open to learning from adults in their lives in a more authentic environment.

An early example of when this may not be the case is when students receive news from peers. Processing and modeling may happen as student peers talk about the news, but it is less likely to be a good example when one news novice models for another. Although modeling is still happening, it may not be the type that helps to develop solid news literacy skills. One advantage, though, is that when news literacy skills are being taught and modeled elsewhere in the student's life, interacting with news and sharing with peers is an opportunity for the student to practice good habits regarding news literacy.

As upper elementary and middle school students begin to establish more of a digital presence, the news messenger may be one more intermediary between the news and the student. That messenger may be an online contact or might be connected only by an acquaintance. In some platforms, such as Twitter, the user may see news that a follower reacted to. Many platforms can be browsed by hashtags or other keywords to find news. In other instances, the app itself will elevate news stories so that they appear in notifications or feeds. When all of these possibilities exist, it can be even more of a challenge for students with an online presence to understand where the news is coming from and how that should affect how they interact with the news. In all of these cases, though, there is a news messenger. Sometimes it may be challenging to identify that messenger. Other times, the challenge may be that the news consumer does not know anything about the messenger. Just as students may view the types of stories that a news broadcaster publishes to better understand the news source, they can also look at the type of stories a particular news messenger shares to see the digital news footprint of that individual or organization.

Besides having an impact on what news we see as news consumers, news messengers can also affect how we react to that news. These messengers may deliver the news with additional commentary, and that commentary can take many forms. It may be a quoted passage of the article, a judgment of agreement or disagreement with the perspective taken within the article, a question to be pondered after engaging with the article, or even simply an emoji. While this can offer clues to give a better understanding of the news messenger, it can also blur the lines of how students should bring their own understanding of the world into making meaning of the news. When a news story is shared, either by a teacher or a distant acquaintance, that news is immediately given some value (whether good or bad) by the student consuming it. When that story is accompanied by commentary that is shared before the student has interacted with the actual piece, it is difficult to view that news without seeing it through the lens of the commentary. That does not mean that the news consumer will always agree with the commentary, just that it is difficult not to be affected by it. This is especially true of our young emerging news consumers.

Have you ever had a conversation with students about a news topic where they were much more opinionated than you thought they would be? For me as an educator, there have been times when those conversations led me to believe that the student was parroting the opinions and reactions of another adult in the student's life. That shouldn't be surprising. As students grow into the role of news consumer, when they are still novices at elements such as reacting to the news, they may take talking points from trusted individuals. Transfer that behavior to news messengers on social media. If students do not know what it means to be a trusted news messenger, what do they do with the varied opinions and reactions that come from the increased number of news messengers in their digital lives? What does parroting that type of behavior look like online? Who can help students navigate any missteps that they may make along the way?

Challenges may be multiplied when the friends who see each other regularly on the playground, class, or after school also share news digitally with each other. Classmates and teammates who are trusted in friendship circles and on the field may not warrant being trusted news messengers. Knowing (and remembering) that we all are not experts at everything, and acting accordingly when it comes to judging others as news messengers, is a complex task and one that students will not immediately master.

Some teachers and parents may be unconcerned. Does it matter if a child is getting misinformation about the newest video game coming out? Is it really a problem if that student shares the information with friends? In the smallest view of that interaction with news, maybe not. But these young learners are establishing strategies to interact with and share information as they become more digitally present. Dismissing the opportunity to teach about news literacy because of the notion that students will figure out good practices on their own is short-sighted at best, and potentially quite harmful.

An August 2019 article from PR Newswire ("News Survey"), which analyzed a Common Sense poll of teens, hints that not all students developing news literacy skills will discover those practices on their own. In that survey of 13- to 17-year-olds, only 53% said that news from social media helped them understand the news event, compared to 65% of teens who got news directly from a news organization. Of those teens using social media for news, 19% reported that their experience actually made them more confused about what was happening. Looking at the role of news messengers on social media may give clues as to why one format for receiving news leaves more teens less informed and confused about the news that they were attempting to learn more about. Students may be receiving more news online, but they are also less likely to be receiving it from trusted news messengers such as educators and parents online. The news that they do receive online comes with varying commentary that alters what they think of the news before they even have the opportunity to interact with the news story. To top it off, the commentary perspectives are varied and not always good models of how to react to the news. It is no wonder teens are left confused. Spending time to focus on news messengers, especially in digital environments, may help alleviate some of that confusion.

These teens, as well as upper elementary and middle school preteens, do need help navigating how they are accessing their news and how to make sense of the messages they receive alongside the news they encounter. They need opportunities to share their own experiences, ask questions, and connect all of this to their learning of news literacy in school.

ORGANIZING FACTS, COMMENTARY, AND PERSONAL REACTIONS

One of the most challenging aspects of teaching news literacy is helping upper elementary and middle school students differentiate between the facts and commentary within the news story, as well as their own personal reactions to both. These are coming from different places: from the news story and from the students themselves. Novices in news literacy can take their own reality and overlay it on the news story, or take up commentary from the story as their own personal reaction. Helping students understand that there are three distinct elements at play—the news report, commentary accompanying the news, and the news consumer's reaction—can help students interpret the news.

Reported news, overall, differs from the news of a century ago or even several decades ago. Most news stories do not contain only facts. There is often commentary from the news reporter or institution that is reporting the news. A May 2019 report from Rand Corporation (Kavanaugh et al., 2019) focused on news in the digital age looks at this shift over the past three decades. The report's analysis of news over that span shows a shift to more subjective reporting. The inclusion of "conversational, argumentative style of news presentation" gives insight into why young people may have difficulty identifying news as news and not something else entirely.

Educators may read the content of the Rand report and think of political news where there are entire channels dedicated to this type of presentation. Although 24-hour news channels may have initiated the style of news reporting heavily interlaced with commentary, it can now be found in all types of news reporting. In its strictest sense, this news reporting is news plus an accompanying element, but it has become much more prevalent in what is accepted in both hard and soft news. For example, a news report on a new gaming system, in addition to the system specifications and release date, may also include commentary about how the system will likely be received or a personal reaction to the quality of the newest games. To our student news consumers, this commentary comes from a trusted news reporter or institution. That could be an individual with a YouTube channel with tens of thousands of followers or a website dedicated to reporting on this particular topic. Because the person or institution is trusted in the reporting of the news, the commentary may also be more likely to be trusted.

I have heard my own students, as they share news that they have recently interacted with outside of school, include the commentary as if it were factual information that had been reported upon. At the same time, the students may also take the commentary from the news report as truth. Essentially, they adopt the accompanying commentary as their own stance.

So what is the problem? I see two. The first is that if students are adopting commentary from the news source, they are abdicating the possibility and responsibility of forming their own opinions. Our students' ability as news consumers to take in information from multiple sources, synthesize it, and react to that found truth is a powerful skill. Borrowing a reaction from another is a poor imitation. The second problem arises when students see the commentary as the news itself. News has the quality of being factual. If students take the accompanying commentary as fact, they may not be open to other commentary (because it does not match an earlier comment) or be left confused and untrusting of the news itself. Discerning the difference between the facts and commentary presented in a news report and knowing that the news consumer's reaction is more than simply what is being reported are powerful tools for students to develop.

The evolution of news reporting as more subjective, conversational, and argumentative in style can lead to news stories that elicit an emotional reaction from the person receiving the news. This is not to say that the news is false or misleading. Instead, it calls for a look at a different understanding of what news is, what accompanies it, and how those who consume the news may need to be prepared to react to it.

It is natural, then, that when the news is presented in a way intended to elicit an emotional reaction, the reaction itself will become part of the process of receiving the news. This reaction on its own is not a bad thing. A story about people in need can create empathy that calls people to action. A report on the newest birth at the local zoo may bring joy and even cause people to connect over that emotional reaction.

It is important, though, that students have experiences that help them separate these three elements. The first step in that process is for students to realize that these elements of interacting with the news exist. Identifying the facts and the commentary within a news story is a beginning step. Later experiences in developing news literacy can explore how facts within a news story support the accompanying commentary. Still other news interactions in the classroom can focus on how news consumers react to news.

As students reflect on their personal reactions to news stories, a place to begin may be with identifying and describing those reactions. This seems like a simple step, but as students work to identify reactions, a rich vocabulary can be tapped into that may draw from literature discussions of character development or social-emotional learning that has taken place in the classroom. Describing those reactions requires a combination of self-awareness and an environment of trust that we hope is being built throughout the learning environment. Tap into these other learning experiences to encourage a depth of description from students. This description could be verbal, written, or even visual. Students could describe connections and questions, as well as emotional or physical reactions to interacting with news stories. Students can also identify what prompted these reactions, both from within the story and their own prior experiences. Equally important is for students to understand that because everyone has prior experiences that they bring to news stories, it would be unlikely that everyone would react the same way to any particular story. This realization helps students move from a well-developed reaction to the news to the possibility of interacting with others about the news in open and nuanced ways. These communal reactions to news based on responses that have emotional roots are often what educators hope for when service learning takes place. This distinction of parts of the news can help currently reported topics play a role in meaningful learning such as service learning.

INSTILLING THE IMPORTANCE OF RELIABILITY AND CREDIBILITY

In some small way, we may be doing our upper elementary and middle school students a disservice when we curate news for them. We, as news messengers, likely garner a fair amount of trust from our students. They trust that when we put a news story in front of them, it is not only important but also from a reliable source and credible. Most educators do not build in time to model the question of whether a news source is trustworthy. It is simply implied, by us delivering it to students, that we have already determined trustworthiness.

What would happen if a student questioned the reliability of a source or the credibility of an article when that was not part of the lesson? I'm afraid there would be more than a few times that the student's question would be pushed aside, because of limited time or even because we may not know how to answer such a question.

The terms *reliability* and *credibility* are often used interchangeably. I describe them as separate terms to my students, and will continue to use that terminology in the lesson later in this book.

When referring to news literacy, the term *reliability* refers to the source that is reporting the news. Some examples would be a newspaper, website, news anchor, television station, YouTube channel, or Twitter handle of a news institution that directly reports news. A measure of the news source's reliability would be a measure of its trustworthiness. How much does the consumer of the news trust the source where the news is coming from? One could also use another measure of reliability when referring to news messengers. For our most novice students on the journey of news literacy, having two separate measurements of reliability may be confusing. Others are further along in their journey, and have developed a strong sense of the reliability of certain news sources and identified the role news messengers play in news consumption. For these students, using reliability as a term to discuss the trustworthiness of both source and messenger can be appropriate.

When speaking of *credibility* in reference to news literacy, look to the news itself. The report will have a degree of credibility or believability. The news report on the dangerous storm that is now coming through town has a high degree of credibility or believability if the person watching the report can look out the window and see the wind and rain. A report about a discovery of alien life would probably have a lower amount of credibility to most news consumers. It would be questioned more and be less believable.

These two measures of news—of the source and the story—can be dependent on each other. If a student believes that a news source is reliable, more credibility is given to the news that the source reports. Likewise, if a student has strong background knowledge on a story and considers a news report to be believable because of that background knowledge, she will likely find the source of that news story more reliable from that one experience with it.

An important point is that reliability and credibility are not set in stone. Both judgments made by news consumers should shift as the consumers become more informed about the news of the day and the sources that provide the news. If I know nothing of a news provider (say, a new website that is reporting on my favorite line of superhero movies), then I should not consider that new source reliable or trustworthy. I have no reason to trust it. But if I continue to see its news confirmed by other reports from trusted websites that I follow, over time the new superhero news site will come to have more reliability with me.

The same can be said of news information and decisions about its credibility. If I know nothing about a news topic, I may not be immediately able to determine whether it is believable or not. The point in these initial judgments, especially if there is a lack of knowledge around a source or a topic, is that we should be driving our news consumption to inform both of these decisions. This can be done in multiple ways. The typical way is to explore outside of that news story. Other news stories on the same or related topics can inform one's understanding of the news event and therefore influence judgments about reliability and credibility. A second way to alter decisions about reliability and credibility is through one's personal experiences with a particular topic.

If I listen to a news report on a YouTube channel about my favorite video game having a major flaw, I may not give it much credibility at first, especially if I've played the game and never seen it myself. Such a news report may be less likely to be believed by me. If I explore and investigate the game more and experience the flaw myself or see a video of someone else experiencing the flaw in the game, the credibility of that original news reporting will be elevated. Of course, the reliability of sources and credibility of news stories can be diminished over time as well.

These judgments on reliability and credibility are unique to individuals. They are dependent on a person's experiences with a news source or with the background knowledge that a news story speaks to. Community judgments about a news source or story can also affect an individual's decisions. If all of my friends have had problems with that same video game, the reading of a news story about it will likely be met with high credibility by me even if I haven't had that same experience.

The hope is that students, and people in general, can come to some general consensus on the reliability and credibility of news sources and news. The importance of the idea that reliability and credibility can be individually determined is that we all bring different experiences to our determinations. Students sharing the understanding that helps them make their determinations can add to a class's collective knowledge about news sources and news itself and help other individuals in the class develop understanding around reliability and credibility and the idea that both can change over time.

My upper elementary students often remember their introductory work about reliable sources and credible information. That learning, taking part largely through a collaborative discussion, is based on their own experiences. These students have experience accessing information and news. They have stories to share about what they look for and how they navigate sources (typically ones online) to find information. It would be extremely unusual, in my experience, to find a student who by fourth or fifth grade had all the considerations about reliable sources and credible information figured out. Collectively, though, any given class of students has had a number of rich experiences that adds up to a solid introductory understanding of evaluating sources and information.

One may ask why this has to be taught. Can't students instead come to their own understandings about reliability and credibility over time? There are several reasons why that wouldn't be advisable. The first is that students' experiences, not only with news and news sources but also in thinking about believability and trustworthiness, varies widely. For some of my students, I am sure our introductory conversation is the first time they have considered these ideas. A second reason is that students also have a wide range of ability to articulate their experiences and thoughts on considerations about reliability of sources and credibility of information. Part of the learning that takes place is establishing an understanding of these ideas, but another important part is a way to articulate those understandings. A third reason is that even the students who have some understanding do not consider reliability and credibility regularly when they interact with the news. As I mentioned, there is a collective initial understanding. This collective understanding is built upon experiences where something did not add up for the students. Typically it was a glaring error on the part of the news source or the news that was reported. But when all seemed well to the students, these ideas were not considered. An important part of incorporating checks on reliability and credibility into news literacy teaching is to have it become an automatic check that all students do whenever they interact with a news source and story.

For many of our upper elementary and middle school students, struggles with reliability and credibility will often not come from misunderstandings about news sources or news stories, but from lack of knowledge of the two. Unless it is a news source that a student interacts with frequently, he or she will likely have no knowledge of it and therefore it will have little reliability with the student.

That is not to say that the source shouldn't be trusted, just that other sources should be referenced as well. The same is true of the news itself. If students are unaware of the context around a news story, they may not know whether to believe a specific news report or not. Instead of dismissing it as unbelievable, students should pose these questions to themselves:

- What do I need to know to understand more about this news story?
- What do I not understand about this news story?
- Is there a trusted source that I could use to learn more?

There are two sets of information that students need to learn as they develop news literacy, one about news and one about themselves. First, regarding the news itself, sources that are reliable and news stories that are credible should be held to a higher value. Second, as consumers of news, students have actions they take to establish that reliability and credibility with news sources and news stories. That call to action—to build toward a greater understanding of the trustworthiness of a news source and the believability of news content—can be a factor that drives students in their work in individual learning opportunities and the greater move toward news literacy.

MAKING SOURCING AND CONTEXTUALIZING AUTOMATIC

There are two important introductory steps for determining reliability and credibility that can be mastered as upper elementary and middle school students encounter news: *sourcing* and *contextualizing*. These are two steps in Stanford History Education Group's Reading Like a Historian skill set.

When sourcing, students take a few moments to identify and connect with as much of the source of the information as possible. When interacting with a news story, they may ask themselves:

- What format is this news story?
- Who created this news story?
- When was the news story created?
- Why would someone tell this news story?
- Who might want to read this news story?

Taking just a minute or two to ask and answer these questions can help students connect to the news story, its purpose, and intended audience. All of this is done without reading, listening to, or watching the news story. Glances at headlines, bylines, and the space surrounding the story begin to inform the news consumer on what the news story is about and lead students to the next step.

As a second step, students take what they have learned from sourcing the news story and contextualize it, making note of the topic on which the source is focused. During contextualizing, students also share what they know about that same topic. Students take all prior knowledge and bring it to the forefront of their minds. This puts them in a position to truly interact with the news at hand and become news consumers. Like sourcing, contextualizing takes only a couple of minutes. This results in an entire introduction to the news story that can be only three to four minutes. As students become more adept at these strategies, they can take even less time. If these skills are used with historical sources, why is it also beneficial to employ these same steps with the news? There are two reasons.

The first reason to teach students to source and contextualize the news is that using a strategy across multiple learning environments (in this case, across news literacy and historical literacy) can help in a variety of ways. It helps students establish those strategies. The more they apply the strategy to different but related situations, the better they will become at performing them independently. Students can begin sourcing and contextualizing sources in age-appropriate ways in early elementary school. Beginning to use these strategies with current and historical news to develop news literacy in upper elementary or middle school should be an easier skill to transfer because of their past experience with it. That can cause less stress for students, take less time for instruction, and give opportunities to teach different content and skills.

As students continue to use sourcing as a strategy in news literacy as they move from upper elementary to middle school, there will continue to be new challenges and experiences. The biggest change may come as they source different formats of news. Sourcing news asks students to be familiar with their news surroundings. Those surroundings change when looking at news on a school-provided website, a reputable news site, a weekly news podcast, or a social media post. Providing students with a variety of formats of news and asking them to use an agreed-upon strategy across all of those sources will continually challenge students. It also teaches them that there are universal ways in which we interact with news. There are stances and activities in the role they take on as news consumers that are the same whether they are reading a newspaper or watching a news video embedded in a tweet.

The second reason to teach sourcing and contextualizing is that these are skills that lead to discussions about reliability and credibility. If a student is sourcing a news story to determine who wrote it and what institution reported it, a natural next question would be, "Do you find that source trustworthy?" In reverse, to answer whether a source of a news story is trustworthy, something must be known about who wrote and published that news story. The same is true of contextualizing. If students are recounting what they know about the topic being reported on in a news story, a logical next question would be, "Is what this news story is reporting believable?" To determine the believability of a news story, students must tap into what they already know about the topic.

These close ties between the sourcing and contextualizing strategies and the questioning of reliability and credibility beg for these strategies, which are often thought of as ones used in history, to be brought into news literacy. The strategies give students a path to address questions of reliability and credibility in a way that they may not otherwise be able to, and help them do so quickly.

Why, then, should students' sourcing and contextualizing be automatic? One reason is that these skills/processes are so intimately connected to discussions of reliability and credibility. Having the first step in that process be an automated one allows students to focus their attention on the more complex tasks of determining the reliability of news sources and the credibility of news stories. Students should also not spend exhaustive amounts of time sourcing and contextualizing news stories. These strategies shouldn't result in paragraphs or pages of student work. In the first lesson of sourcing a news source and contextualizing a news topic, students may spend just a few minutes performing each task. With practice, that time should be shortened. As students master and internalize these skills, the time they spend will be measured in seconds, not minutes. This doesn't mean that they can verbalize their thinking in that short a time. Regularly building formative checks into students' interactions with news literacy can give students additional practice in making their thinking visible and teachers insight into students' nimbleness in performing these strategies with a variety of news topics and formats.

For that mastery to happen, students must be regularly exposed to news stories every school year. Sourcing and contextualizing should regularly be present in some form. As the skills are mastered, the time it takes to apply them becomes negligible. This collective effort can take place over years. The leadership of a school librarian, reading specialists, curriculum coordinator, or administrator can help bridge these expectations over the years and buildings as classroom teachers work together to establish this regular exposure.

ABANDONING OLD APPROACHES TO INFORMATION AND NEWS LITERACY

If you are reading this book, you are probably also familiar with other methods of teaching news literacy and information literacy. There are two general methods that I think should be abandoned entirely. The first is teaching information or news literacy through entirely fictitious sites. The second is teaching news literacy through the use of acronyms that signify a series of questions.

The first, the use of fictitious sites, may be used more often in general information literacy lessons but attempts to target some of the same skills that are part of building news literacy. You may be familiar with the website about the Pacific Northwest Tree Octopus (https://zapatopi.net/treeoctopus), a site about a fictional creature. This is one of the better known examples of fictitious sites. The site, created in 1998, has been widely used in literacy studies because it has many features found on reliable websites and goes to great lengths to convince the reader that the content on the site is real.

What I have read or heard teachers share about why they use this site with students can ultimately be summed up as a lesson that not everything on the internet can be believed. Unfortunately, a deeper look at how students often interact with the website often reveals that students do not use the news literacy skills of sourcing and contextualizing and asking questions about the source's reliability and the information's credibility. Students who struggle to determine whether these sites share fictitious information may not ask questions about the origin of the information, reflect on any context they have prior knowledge of, and use those pieces of information to ask whether the site itself seems trustworthy or the information appears to be believable.

Those are valuable skills to practice. But why not do that reflecting with actual news sites? Whether using sites that have curated news for upper elementary and middle school students or publicly used news sites, the same desired skills can be practiced.

The possible reason fictitious sites have been used to teach news or information literacy in classrooms and libraries is that they have been used in studies. Although the focus and methods of the studies vary, one constant that people often draw from these experiments is that many young people do not thoroughly question sources of information or compare the information with existing knowledge. Donal Leu, the John and Marie Neag Endowed Chair in Literacy and Technology at the University of Connecticut, who ran a study using the Tree Octopus website, seems to agree in a 2016 interview: "They [students] do not know how to locate information or evaluate information, and they do not know how to communicate information in a richer context beyond text messaging."

It is unclear whether educators use these sites to recreate the study, hope their students will do better than the study findings, or some other reason. What is clear is that lessons using this site and others like it put many students in a "gotcha" situation. If the teacher presents the site as reputable or the topic as a credible one to research, only later to show them that everything they have seen is false, then the educator has misrepresented not only the site, but also himself or herself. Teachers work to present themselves as trusted providers of information—informed messengers—but then purposely give students disinformation. It is no wonder that many students trust their teachers and do not question the source itself. Instead of these "gotcha" teaching moments, we should be working on news and information literacy skills with actual news and information that is not meant to trick or fool students.

One may also ask why students do not go beyond the site itself to search for more information. This skill of leaving the information or news source to verify information within it is important. This skill has been highlighted by many, maybe most notably the Stanford History Education Group (n.d.). If the skill is so critical, why is it often not used with the lessons involving these types of sites? I see two possible reasons. One is that the students have not yet been taught this skill. It has not been modeled for them and has not become part of a regular thinking routine. Another returns to the earlier point: that the lesson itself is often introduced with the teacher, a trusted messenger, presenting the topic and source as credible. In a sense, students are being asked to question the teacher's authority as an expert on information and then to question what they are reading. It is no wonder that some students do not naturally do that.

A related reason that teachers may use this site and similar sites with students is out of a fear that students will be tricked or duped by disinformation. This fear of fake information and fake news may cause educators to replicate those interactions in an attempt to warn students of the dangers of the internet. Surely it is important for students to be able to identify intentional disinformation that they find online. However, I argue that this shouldn't be the initial focus of news and information literacy teaching. Instead, students' ability to question the credibility of the information they interact with, to identify misinformation and disinformation, and to be wary of that disinformation should be the result of a solid foundation in news and information literacy.

It is likely that the majority of news that students interact with does not intentionally attempt to mislead them with disinformation. There are other types of information to be wary of, though, including advertisements that attempt to look like news, news commentary that may appear to be news, or omission of information from a news report. Experiences that build strong news literacy skills help students identify these moments when it is important to question the information that is put in front of them. It also prepares them to ask questions and look for information that will help them identify disinformation. For a variety of reasons, these fictitious sources should not be used to teach news and information literacy. Instead, use actual news and authentic information sources. Use them often and purposefully.

A second practice in news and information literacy that should be abandoned are methods that rely on multistep evaluative processes to evaluate sources; many are wrapped up in somewhat memorable acronyms such as the CRAAP Test. These packaged news analysis tools, also used in information literacy circles, do have some redeeming qualities. Primarily, they encourage students not to accept the first source they find as completely appropriate to their needs and reliable.

Healthy skepticism before fully investing in sources is a good thing, but there are several missteps built in these acronym protocols that students are asked to use. First, time and discomfort are an obstacle. Is the goal to have students look at one source through five or more lenses, where each of those lenses has multiple questions to address before that one source passes muster? If so, those students are in for a long and painful experience when interacting with possibly dozens of sources for a large project. Long and painful experiences are not usually taken up willingly. Expect students to abandon the acronym method as soon as they can.

Other concerns I have about teaching news and information literacy through the use of acronym tools include:

- They seem very black-and-white. Students, when growing as news literate individuals, need opportunities to say, "I don't know," and then focus their attention on what they do know. That isn't to say that lessons can't focus students' attention on growing skills and knowledge that will add tools to how they interact with news. But when I use every tool I have in determining if a source is valuable or legitimate for my needs, what happens when I have one "no" and the rest "yes"? Do I use the source? Where is the tipping point? These acronym marathons do not tell us, and I have not heard valuable advice from those who use them.

- There are too many steps. No one can realistically be asked to answer what could be a series of 20 or more questions about one source before even determining whether it should be used for learning. When used for news literacy, the news itself is practically old news by the time students are done with this first step. What we should do instead is help students identify what is uniquely important to look more closely at with particular pieces of news and information to determine a source's value. That certainly is a more nuanced approach and asks students to spend more time away from that one source.

- They are too focused on the source. How can this be a bad thing? As I wrote earlier, Stanford History Education Group has widely shown that those who best identify misleading news and information very quickly go outside of the initial source to compare it with information elsewhere. The news literate use sources they know and trust to quickly identify whether a source is reliable and its information is credible. Certainly, looking at URLs is important, along with understanding a source's perspective and a host of other information that can be found at the source itself. However, more time should be spent looking at other sources on the same topic so students gain context and understanding that they can bring to their analysis of the news source and the information it provides.

- Acronym protocols are not focused enough on the user of the source. One major element that I think such protocols ignore is the users themselves. The students who are interacting with information are not robots that process the news and information and then move on. They can be emotionally affected by it and they also bring their own reality to it. This is one reason we do not all react to any piece of news in the same way. To be objective, though, students should not only want to critically look at news and the information it shares, they should also look critically at themselves. What understanding do they bring to a news story? What emotions are sparked by it? What questions is the news eliciting from me? Ignoring these elements concerning the news consumer does not give students a full perspective of the value of a given news story to them as individuals.
- These protocols are too linear. This may be a criticism of how these tools are used rather than their intended use. Use of these screeners to determine whether a news or information source passes the test often takes place early in the information-gathering process. Then the source is checked off the list and not heard from again. However, as a student's understanding of a topic grows, it may become apparent through the many layers of questions and answers in one of these tests that there is new information to be considered. As related to the earlier criticism of the test being too black-and-white, if the initial results are murky and grey, might a student return to the source to consider its value after gaining new contextual knowledge about the topic? Of course. Students' interactions with information, including news, should be a circular path as they become more informed and can give new considerations to a given piece of information. If the process of evaluating sources simply consists of checking many questions off a list, this is unlikely to happen.

The lessons in this book do not point to fictitious news to put students in "gotcha" moments. Students will not learn an acronym to use every time they read, watch, or listen to a news story. What the book attempts to do through the series of lessons set out in Chapter 4 is expose students to different ways to interact with and view information and themselves when they are taking in the news. There is no specific correct order in which to implement these lessons, although they have been grouped and some lessons rely upon previously learned skills. Those skills may have already been developed through other learning, either in news literacy or informational literacy lessons. Feel free to adapt the content to meet your needs. These lessons are intended to be the beginning of what will ultimately be a lifelong activity, as students experience the news, gain news literacy skills through the lessons, and then go beyond the walls of your classroom or library to use those skills as they encounter news.

3

News Literacy: Tying Together Multiple Literacies Across Subjects

It would certainly be convenient if, in our efforts to teach news literacy, we were truly dealing with only one type of literacy. Of course, we know that isn't so. One of the ways we know this is that news stories come to consumers of news in so many ways. I have a dear friend who still has the local newspaper delivered to her house (I do not know many others who do). When she sees a story that she wants to share, she takes a photo of it with her phone and posts it on social media along with her commentary. Another friend only listens to news in the car while driving. A third typically watches clips on his phone. The formats alone necessitate different literacies.

Educators must hope that students will have experiences with analyzing print, audio, and video formats from an early age. When students are exposed to new content, specifically news content, educators may find that students need additional support even though they are interacting with formats they may already be familiar with. Being able to meet those students' learning needs will also call for educators to be able to identify the literacies that come into play.

NEWS LITERACY: MADE UP OF MANY PARTS

Although this book does not designate lessons as addressing specific literacies, an effort is made to include different literacies within the resources being used across lessons. Knowing that educators will likely substitute content to meet their curricular needs, teachers and librarians are encouraged to consider continually exposing students to the different literacies that make up the whole of news literacy. The following list is by no means exhaustive but could be considered when selecting news stories and making decisions about how students will interact with them.

Text Literacy

Part of traditional literacy, *text literacy*—being able to read and make meaning from what they read—is how many students receive most of their instruction related to news literacy. Reading the news can be challenging, though. With new news every day, there is also the likelihood of new content and vocabulary for young learners of news literacy skills. Those who struggle with text literacy may find it difficult to focus on developing other literacies, using analysis skills, and reflecting on their interactions with the news.

There are ways that educators can support students in building text literacy, even while students develop other news literacy skills. First, consider encouraging students to interact with different formats of news on the same topic. This does not mean abandoning text. Instead, much of the news today has text support embedded within it. As students watch televised or web news broadcasts, students can often have closed captioning turned on to support the reading of the news along with the visual and auditory interactions. Being able to hear the words spoken while reading, as well as having visual images to support the written news, can be a boost for those who struggle with text literacy.

Newspapers and other written news are typically written at a middle school reading level. This can reassure some students that they will be able to work through the text. For others, it can be disheartening. Consider news sources that are targeted to young learners in upper elementary and middle school. These written news resources, both in print and online, may give information about reading levels or, when online, even adapt the news story to target a reader's instructional or independent reading level.

When working with news created for a wider audience, in addition to exploring the multiple formats described earlier, consider gathering a variety of news reports on the same topic. Story teasers used by news sources when sharing on social media are another source of story overviews or "hooks" that students can use. These one or two sentences can provide context and introduce vocabulary that students can use when reading a complete story. Having a variety of article lengths, story structure, contextual text, and vocabulary gives options for a diverse pool of readers.

When my students work with historically based news, this idea of providing a variety of sources for students to interact with plays a role in engaging all students in the text. Headlines, captions, and articles of varied lengths are all used to provide context to all readers. As I share gathered articles, I typically encourage students to choose their own. After introducing the topic, I share the articles in print or digitally, making sure that students can see the full scope of the article they are selecting. I read through the headlines, encouraging students to select one that they want to explore further. Students will gravitate to resources that they feel comfortable navigating.

In addition to choice, I give my students guidance in how they will be interacting with the text before they select the news story they will interact with. Students who may be considered striving readers may select a more challenging text if they are confident in the strategy used to interact with that text. I'll provide brief descriptions of possible analysis strategies later in this chapter as I connect news literacy skills to historical thinking skills. These strategies are explored in depth in Chapter 4.

There is an added benefit of choice. If you allow your students to select from a finite number of preselected print articles of varying lengths but on the same topic, you can be assured that none of them will be exactly the same. Different details will be covered. Possibly different perspectives will be explored. One news story may contain updates because it was published hours or even days later. This allows each article to provide different news literacy experiences to the students who read them. These varied experiences are important for one reason that is critical to students' building of news literacy skills: collaboration.

When students collaborate, they gain the collective support of the class in building their own news literacy. Specifically with text-based news, students reading from different news articles come to a collaboration with slightly different information on the same news topic. I do not have to worry about whether my striving readers have something unique to contribute. More importantly, they do not have to be concerned about that either, because there will be something unique in the article that they read. Yes, there may be a limited number of others who have read the same article depending on the number of news stories I provide, but different strategies allow for different types of collaborative sharing which can assure that students have individual opportunities to contribute to the collective understanding of the news topic.

Most students can also benefit from vocabulary support as they experience new content. As teachers preview news articles that will be shared with students or prepare for students to search for their own news stories on specific news topics, they can anticipate vocabulary that students may struggle with. Providing a teacher-created glossary for a news article is one option that can support students' interactions with written news. This option may also streamline students' interactions with text if time is a factor and give student-friendly definitions. For a more collaborative experience, some classrooms keep an ever-evolving classroom glossary. Students submit to the glossary words that they read for assignments, read for pleasure, or encounter outside of the school day. Structures vary, but students work together to find definitions and adapt them to make them friendly and accessible to all students in the class. These types of classroom glossaries can exist in the classroom but may be most collaborative when created and accessed digitally through a shared document that all students edit and view. Another technology-focused approach is to have students read their news entirely online, allowing them to access dictionary support directly within browsers and other applications by simply right-clicking or control-clicking on a word they need to have defined.

As a librarian, I may rely on the expertise of classroom teachers when it comes to vocabulary support. Not only can teachers share what type of vocabulary instruction students are already acquainted with, they may also have insight into specific vocabulary within a news story or topic that students are already familiar with or are likely to struggle with. This does not mean that the librarian must always defer to the classroom teacher. A partnership should be established. For example, if librarians have an understanding about how new vocabulary is addressed differently in other classrooms or later grade levels, they may work with classroom teachers to implement this same support with news literacy instruction. If the librarian sees stellar instruction in a classroom around vocabulary that moves students from passive to active supporters of their own vocabulary development, the librarian can elevate that teacher's work and share it with others in the school or even the district.

As students read news articles, consider how they would interact with other text, especially other nonfiction texts, in your classroom or library. Many of these same reading strategies can be incorporated into their reading of the news. Strategies may be adaptations of those used when reading other fiction or nonfiction; these might include:

- Recognizing the structure of the news story and using it to preview the content.
- Identifying the person, group, or other item of focus in the news story.
- Understanding the key action or problem being reported.
- Summarizing the news article.
- Predicting future elements or asking questions based on an overall understanding of the report.

These focus areas can be introduced, reinforced, or revisited with written news reports.

Visual Literacy

A picture is worth a thousand words. But if students lack the visual literacy skills to be able to "read" a photograph, pictures can be overlooked and students may miss the opportunity to add to their understanding of the news story. Developing those visual literacy skills while interacting with news gives students a variety of ways to connect with their world through photographs.

In the news, photographs typically accompany a written story. There are times when they are also shown briefly as part of a video news report. In either case, make it a point to direct students' attention to the photographs within a news story. It may be helpful to begin with them, not only as a way to build context for students before they read text or listen to a news report, but also as a prompt for students to begin asking questions as part of their interactions with the news story. Beginning with photographs also elevates those elements as integral parts of the news article or report. These visuals are not an addition to a news story. They are part of that story.

There are two main actions for students when interacting with a photograph: observing it and reacting to it. These two actions do not have to happen in any particular order. People often do these things simultaneously as they interact with visuals. As students develop visual literacy skills, it may be helpful to target their attention toward making observations and then transitioning to reacting and asking questions.

Educators can craft their initial prompts for engaging students with news photographs to guide students through making observations regarding those photographs. Each of these questions targets the student's attention on the photograph itself and how the student can share those observations with others. Students may notice different elements of the photograph or may choose to talk about different aspects of it. Questions to target students' attention to making observations include:

- What do you see?
- What do you see that makes you say that?
- What seems important in this photograph?
- Is there a caption that can tell us more about this photo?

In addition to observing, students should react to the photo. Students make meaning from visual images through these two tasks, observing and reacting. Students may actually begin by reacting to the image, sharing what they think is happening, or inferring how someone feels or what that person is thinking. If no one has yet verbalized the observation that the reaction is based on, teachers can ask students to share what they saw that made them think this. Other question prompts can encourage students to react to the photo in a news story and begin to interpret the captured moment. Such questions include:

- What do you think is happening in this photograph?
- What do you think the photographer wanted us to notice in this photo?
- What could the people in this photograph be saying or thinking?
- How might this person be feeling?

This opportunity to interpret emotions can be an important one in "reading" a news photograph. Images can contain individuals from different perspectives and therefore have many emotions portrayed. It is important for students to know that their descriptions of the emotions being shown in a news photograph are reactions and not direct observations. When the local news reports a story of people helping to clean up the state park on Earth Day, the accompanying photo could elicit varying descriptions of the volunteers. "Happy," "determined," or "thoughtful" could all be used to describe the people in the photo. These words are all very different, though. This is because students are interpreting the photograph differently.

There are three elements that often play a role in students' interpretation of a news photograph. The first are observations of the photo itself. Students may base their emotional description on facial expressions, body language, and even the surroundings. Also, though students should all be able to agree on what they see in a news photograph, certain elements may be determined to be more important by some students. For example, for one student, the facial expression may be the driving factor in describing the emotion. For another, it may be the surroundings in which the person is set.

The second element that can help students interpret the emotions of individuals in a news photograph is the news topic itself. Knowing as much about the story as possible can help students interpret the photo that is a visual representation of that story.

The third element that students may use to interpret emotions within a news photograph is their own background knowledge. When I've spoken with students who make this type of connection, I find there is some element of the photograph that they have observed that they connect with an event in their own life. These connections may be extremely concrete or completely abstract. Students sometimes have trouble initially explaining the connection.

I think it is important to note that the background knowledge that students utilize when interpreting photos may cause them to misinterpret the emotions in the photograph. I remember a news photograph of an Olympic runner who had just won a marathon. He was being propped up at the end of the race, exhausted, face slack. One student who expressed a strong dislike for running was certain that the Olympic marathon runner was displeased and unhappy. He had made a connection with what he saw in the news photo, but had misinterpreted it based on his own experiences. We work to develop a holistic look at news literacy by developing supporting literacies such as visual literacy. Although I could have talked through why I didn't think an Olympic marathon winner would be unhappy with his results, I chose to let collaboration and other literacies speak to the student's interpretation. Other students appropriately disagreed with his interpretation and shared why. Later we looked at the accompanying news article so the students had a broader look at the moment than the photograph could provide, including an interview with the marathon winner. This student was able to correctly interpret the emotional feelings of the person in the news story after reading through the text of the news story. This is one example where the experience of interacting with news, instead of the teacher, can help a student develop personal news literacy skills.

As to these last two elements, prior knowledge of the news story and personal connection to the photograph, I have found that students sometimes have limited or no connections and are relying strictly on observations. If lack of knowledge of the news topic is a concern, consider taking time to focus on visuals of news stories after students have interacted with other text, video, or audio in a story. Reading just a headline and a caption can sometimes give enough knowledge of the topic to allow deeper exploration of a photograph. If a teacher is hoping that students can connect their own background knowledge to emotionally interpret a photograph, the teacher may ask pointed questions to target students' reflection toward their own lives.

Interpreting visual images does not have to be solely responding to a series of questions. Students can use a "jump-in" strategy where they imagine themselves in a photograph or as a person in a photograph to make their observations. This type of strategy encourages interpretation as students use their imagination, based on what they see and their own background knowledge, to take a split second captured in a photograph and expand it to a moment that is reported in a news story.

Remember that these strategies to connect and react to visual images are not the final step in interacting with a news story. Though they can help a student connect to a news image, personal connections can also lead to unintentional misinterpretations. Continuing to interact with the rest of the news story can address any misconceptions.

Audiovisual Literacy

Audiovisual news is a powerful medium for sharing the news. It conveys two factors that other forms of news media sometimes do not portray as well: motion and emotion. Even compared to a visual news image, news footage can often better portray emotion. Not only are the visuals of body language and facial expression telling, but a speaker's voice can also help students determine an individual's emotions. Seeing the motion of a moment within a news story may help students understand that moment better. As more than a snapshot in time, lengths of video or film can reveal more to the viewer than a still photo. To look at earlier examples around news stories concerning video games or movies, seeing and hearing either within the context of a news story can give the student a better feel for what is being reported. With news that may be more likely to be explored in the classroom, news footage of local volunteers in action gives students a better understanding of what volunteerism looks like in a particular instance. These types of visual elements in news can be especially helpful when students lack context or are unfamiliar with a news topic. What is sometimes described as "B-roll footage"—supplemental news footage that is added to the primary video footage for a news story—can be essential in setting context for news viewers, especially those with limited knowledge of the topic. While the primary footage may be a person being interviewed or a reporter reading news prompts, the B roll shows a visual representation of the news story. In a historical news context, students studying school desegregation may watch B-roll footage of protesters outside schools in the 1950s. In this instance, the footage can be paired with interviews. The additional footage shows, through its motion and scope, the number of people and the movement and reaction at different points within a crowd. Beyond the interview itself, this type of footage can not only affect students' understandings of an event but also cause emotional reactions.

One useful strategy is to focus on this type of B-roll footage. When my students analyze news footage that has an element of motion, they can use a variety of annotation techniques. One is to rely on question prompts similar to analysis of other news formats. Students may respond to:

- What movement do you notice in the news footage?
- How does that movement help you understand the moment being captured?
- What word or short phrase could you use to describe the movement?

Another annotation strategy that students can use to interact with motion within a news video is to sketch what they see in the video. Arrows or lines can be used to show motion or movement within the sketched news scene. When my students use this method, I pay particular attention to what they include and what they leave out of their sketches. Given the movement within a scene, students will not be able to capture everything. I take note of what moment they decided to capture and what details were included. This can give me insight into where they focused their attention in the news footage. This focus could be caused by many things. They could have questions, an emotional reaction, or a personal connection. The sketch can provide a starting point to help them further articulate that connection to have a more meaningful interaction with the news story.

The motion within audiovisual clips can help students understand the tempo or rhythm of a location, especially one that is unknown to them. Many are able to "put themselves in the scene" being shown in the news clip and thus appreciate the scope of the story. Encouraging students, through analysis and discussion, to make meaning from these movements and images can be a powerful tool that they can pair with the written and spoken words of a news report to gain an understanding of an individual or event in the news.

Specifically prompt students with:

- What do you see that is new to you?
- What does this place remind you of?
- What did you see in the video that you didn't expect to see?
- What did you expect to see in the video that you did not see?
- What is happening in the video that the words are not telling us?

These questions can focus student attention on the visuals of a news story. Some of these questions also help students make connections between their own experiences and the news topic as students share what they are reminded of or what is new to them. If the educator wants to tap into prior experiences with the news topic or news reporting, questions about expectations may help students make connections with recent interactions with a particular news topic regardless of the format. Presenting this question before students view the news report can also prompt them to make predictions. Finally, asking students to compare the visuals in a news story to the written or spoken word can help students break down a more complex storytelling format and perform close readings or viewings of each individual part.

Movement, which is not seen in historical news, may also make modern-day news feel cluttered or distracting. Headlines scrolling across the bottom of the screen, moving graphics framing the reporting, and more information on the topic ticking down a sidebar can be overwhelming to anyone, especially those developing news literacy skills. Helping students target their attention on one element of the screen at a time through the use of a structured analysis method can focus their information gathering. As most upper elementary or middle school students will not watch this type of news during a live broadcast, but rather as a clip available online, they will have the benefit of watching, rewatching, and pausing the report if they want. Incorporating this ability for students to control their own viewing of a news report, even one being used as part of a lesson, is an empowering consideration that students can utilize outside of school to fully take in a news report.

Audiovisual news reports often include "talking heads." The term has the connotation of being disinteresting, but in such instances sound and movement may play a very important role of conveying emotion. Interviews and panel discussions are not considered action-packed, but compared to a transcript of the same text, they are rich with additional meaning. Inflection, tone, and pacing can give viewers an impression of the feelings of the speaker. Body language and facial expressions add even more to the viewer's understanding of the layers of meaning on top of the words that are spoken. To help students realize this, think about breaking a short news video of an interview down into its component parts. Ask students to watch the news report with no sound. Then, if possible, provide a transcript or closed captioning, also with no sound. Third, layer in the sound of the news story. For each passing view, students can make new observations, reactions, and questions to the news topic being reported. Initially ignoring the words being spoken and focusing on other visual or auditory aspects can reveal additional meanings for students.

This skill of listening for additional meaning beyond the text becomes even more important when students are solely listening to the news. The news may be listened to over the radio or podcast, or students may be multitasking and listening to a video clip. In addition to listening to the voice of the person reporting or the individual being interviewed, there may be other sounds that can help students increase their understanding. The constant clicking of cameras during an interview of a sports figure conveys the importance of the person or event. A variety of voices or sounds behind a person being interviewed gives some idea of the surroundings. Although the strategy is not used as a lesson in this book, students can simply close their eyes and listen to a news clip, with directions to share what they hear and how that affects their understanding of the news story.

Graphic and Geographic Literacy

Graphic and geographic literacy seem to lend themselves to math and social studies instruction throughout elementary and middle school more than to news literacy objectives. While they may only be seen in selective news reports, students will come across graphs, tables, and charts when reading or watching the news. Maps and geographic references are mentioned frequently in a variety of news stories. Reading, understanding, and making meaning from graphs, tables, and charts, as well as maps, in the news gives students real-world uses for these literacies.

Graphical Literacy

Graphical literacy can sometimes be extended over time. A news report may take numeric data from one moment in time and represent it graphically. It also can take data from across time leading up to the moment of the news report. That could show itself in temperature changes over a day, attendance records at a local event over the course of a week, or price changes for the last quarter or year. If numerical data can be represented in the news graphically to show the present and past, students can be challenged to predict future trends. Students can also follow news stories over time to track changes that are graphically displayed.

That literacy of reading and making meaning from graphs, tables, and charts can be extended from what is taught and mastered in math when found in news reports. Prompts can encourage students to take that meaning and extend their thinking. They may be asked:

- If this current and past information is true, what can we predict may happen in the future?
- What variables may have had an impact on the information we see in this graph/table/chart?
- Given this data, what decision would you make going forward? Why?
- Given this data, what is your opinion of the decision of the person/people focused on in the news report?

Many of these questions require subjective answers, as they ask students to take graphical information, other information from the news report, and possibly their own background knowledge to formulate a response. As teachers consider assessing student graphical literacy as a subset of news literacy or set learning objectives in place, the goal students are striving for is the skill of bringing these multiple understandings together to convey and support a full comprehension.

If educators wish to add another layer of complexity to enhance graphical literacy, have students pursue graphical representations of news being reported. Reading a news story about opening-weekend box office numbers for a new movie release may cause a student to seek out a table of prior weeks. Another may look for information about movies released during the same time in earlier years. If a report has historic numbers, a student may look for graphs of top opening movie weekends of all time.

All of the searches in this example have a common thread in that the searches help to put the news into a larger context. But each search also serves a different purpose when comparing news of today to past news. How does this movie news compare to the small moment of the past weeks, to the larger moment of the same release time over years, or to the best movies of all time? Depending on how students want to interact with the news, they may seek out different graphical information. But couldn't this all be found in other news stories? Yes—so why seek out graphical news to answer these types of questions? Simply put, graphical representation of some news provides a quick answer with numerically based information.

As students process, interpret, and connect the news with the world, they may also consider taking lessons from graphical representations of the news. Graphs, tables, and charts found in the news can be used as models as students work to organize and make meaning of data-rich information within the news. Data across multiple related news stories can be brought together by students and represented in ways that are similar to what is shown in news reports.

In addition to graphing data within news stories, students may also find it informative to graph the news stories themselves. Tracking how often and when a news topic was reported within a newspaper can provide a numeric representation of the importance of the news topic. These tracking methods can be done with multiple searches through historical news sites or ongoing tracking for current news stories.

Geographic Literacy

Whether students are reading, viewing, or listening to news from their home town, state, country, or news that is covering a world event, locations are likely mentioned. In the local reporting, a nearby neighborhood or street may be mentioned. Regional news at the state level may reference a neighboring town or regional vacation spot. National news could highlight a natural disaster in a neighboring state or a sporting event taking place halfway across the country. World news could share a scientific breakthrough reported by a team of researchers in another country. The point is that all news takes place somewhere. When we ask students not only to make sense of the news but also to understand the greater context around it, an understanding of where the news is taking place can be important.

Geographic understanding of a news story may also affect how a student reacts to the news. Knowing prior related news that is connected to the same geographic location may cause a more nuanced reaction or influence the questions that are asked. If students outside the state of California have some understanding that wildfires are regular occurrences there, news of wildfires may not seem shocking. It may, however, cause them to ask questions about how current wildfires compare to years past in severity, location within the state, or time of year. Without a geographic understanding of the area and the news that is attached to it, those types of questions would likely not be asked.

Knowing geography, then, is an important part of geographic literacy. Student interactions with maps and globes, both offline and online, are meaningful beginning steps. But when it comes to news literacy, knowing the news that is attached to that geography also becomes valuable for fully interacting with the news through a geographic lens. How does a connection between geography and news develop? It is a slow and deliberate process.

- Prompt students to contextualize a location when preparing to read a news story.
- Intentionally reference geographic locations when discussing a news story.
- Encourage students to interact with a map in relation to a news story.
- When maps are incorporated into visual news broadcasts, ask students to interact with them as part of their news analysis.
- Look for news stories that take place not only over time but also over geographic space. Use digital mapping tools to document where parts of the news story are taking place.
- Approach the analysis of historical news through a geographic lens to focus on geographic literacy.

There is no single approach for building graphic and geographic literacy as part of the broader picture of news literacy. One challenge is certain, though: These literacies cannot be built quickly. An ongoing approach over years of an upper elementary and middle school student's learning can have a positive impact.

COMPARING NEWS LITERACY TO HISTORICAL LITERACY

I will admit that I look at most information through a historical lens. My training has led me to look carefully at historical items and how students can make meaning from them. That is often done through collaborative analysis using a variety of tools.

Newspapers are frequently used as primary sources when bringing together resources to understand history. If we consider a primary source to be an item or object directly connected with a topic of study and a related time period, then newspapers, news broadcasts, and any other news media fit that bill. News, by the definition earlier in the book, is time sensitive regarding the event it is reporting about. This means that if a topic of study has been reported on in the news, that news report becomes a primary source of the event. Thus, all news reports have the potential of also being primary sources, depending on students' focus of study. In a more historical sense, as soon as a news event has passed, the news becomes historical news as well as a historical record of the moment.

If all news can thus be considered primary sources regarding the events they report on, then using the same historical thinking skills with primary sources that develop historical literacy should develop news literacy. Those historical thinking skills must be flexible enough to adapt to the many formats of news.

This book uses several strategies within the lessons typically employed to develop historical literacy as it also develops news literacy. Sourcing and contextualizing are used as an introductory strategy when first interacting with a news source. When sourcing, students are asked to briefly look at the news source and determine some basic information about that source. When used with historical documents, students may be asked why a certain format was created. When sourcing exclusively news sources, part, if not all, of that answer will be "to inform." Questions about sourcing would include questions about the person who created or delivered the news story and the organization that published it. In current news found on social media, one would also consider what is known about the news messenger who shared it. Taking a moment to discover the topic of the news story is also part of sourcing because it is used in contextualizing.

Contextualizing takes the topic of the news story and asks students what they already know about that topic or related topics. Two to three minutes to think about and discuss what they know about a news topic before they read the news story is an important step. It brings what students know to the forefront and prepares them to actively engage with a news story. Contextualizing encourages students to engage with the news and not just consume it.

These two tasks, sourcing and contextualizing, prepare students to interact with both historical documents and current news. When interacting with the historical item itself, I am asking students to do three things: make observations, react to those observations, and ask questions. Their own background knowledge plays a key role in how students react and question and even in what they observe. This is why contextualizing—bringing that background knowledge to the forefront—is so crucial. By observing, reacting, and questioning, students develop some level of understanding of the historical document they are interacting with. There are many different analysis methods to achieve these three steps, but at their core these are the interactions I want students to engage in.

Compare those interactions to interactions with the news for a moment. When my students are working with current news, I want them to *observe* every part of it. That may be by listening, reading, watching, or a combination of the three mediums. My hope is that they take in as much of the content of that news as possible. I know that their prior experience with that news topic, or lack thereof, affects what they observe. My students should react to the news. How does the news make them feel? What do they think of the events or the people involved? All of the observations and reactions should lead to questions. I think this is one of the most important type of interactions with news because it acknowledges that a student's interaction with the news does not stop with her or his reaction to it. Questions necessitate answers. Finding those answers means seeking out credible information from reliable sources.

One specific strategy that incorporates observation, reaction, and questioning is a *close reading* strategy. Many lessons in this book ask students to give a close reading to a news report. Here, students read through a lens that asks them to focus their attention on one element of the news story. With the broad scope of many news stories, reading through a lens targets students' attention as they interact with the news story. For my students, it also encourages reactions and questions based on the lens through which they are viewing the story. A close reading of news asks students to do more than just understand the words or, more broadly, the events on the page or the screen. It asks them, through the analysis process, to interact, to look for patterns, to make meaning from the story itself. Even though "reading" is in its name, the strategy can also be used with broadcast news and incorporate both visuals and text.

Another important strategy that is used in several lessons is *corroboration*. For corroboration, students read several other news stories to confirm the information reported in an initial news account. This is where students developing their own questions as part of interacting with news is key. Although it is important to reach beyond one news story to confirm information across reports, students may question that importance. Their own queries become the reasoning for exploring related news stories. Corroboration becomes a secondary but equally important task for the student. The strategies of corroborating information and answering questions work well together. When confirming content within a news story, we wouldn't expect one news story to be an exact copy of another. Each will likely have some unique elements and, we hope, overlapping information that can be confirmed. The reliability or trustworthiness of the news source is important to this strategy of analyzing additional news to corroborate initial findings.

These strategies and others help students to pull the information from the news, interact with it, and make meaning from it, much like what they are used to doing to develop historical literacy. Similar to historical literacy, there is a desire to prepare to interact with the news, to interact with the news in meaningful ways, and then to go beyond that news both to confirm the reporting and to explore the news event further. This compatibility of strategies and skills in the development of news literacy and historical literacy is one of the reasons that the lessons within this book focus on both historical news and modern news.

NEWS LITERACY ACROSS THE SUBJECT AREAS

The phrase "news literacy" may not be found in your school's or district's curriculum. Keywords that anchor this book and the lessons within it may not either. With overpacked curriculums and schedules, the question may be asked, "Where do I fit news literacy into the day?" The simplest answer is "everywhere." As students are asked in lessons throughout this book to view the news through a particular lens, teachers can challenge themselves to view their curriculum, both content and skills, through the lessons of this book.

Many may consider the most natural connections to be those happening with social studies lessons. History lessons likely have news stories that document curricular topics of study similar to topics explored in this book. Although the lessons in this book are intended to focus on news around different historical topics, there was also an effort to vary the moments in history explored through these news literacy lessons. The historical topics outlined in this book include:

- The 1859 incident at Harper's Ferry
- Civil War ballooning
- The Alaska Gold Rush of the 1890s
- Halloween pranks in the early twentieth century
- The 1912 sinking of the *Titanic*
- Nell Burke's and Alice Richardson's 1916 suffrage drive across the United States
- The 1917 sinking of the *Algonquin*
- A letter from a WWI soldier published in a local paper
- Mass unemployment in 1931
- The Dust Bowl of the 1930s
- The 1941 attack on Pearl Harbor
- The 1956 Jim Crow bus boycott
- The 1963 Birmingham campaign
- June 1979 gasoline shortages
- 1989 recycling efforts in Seattle
- A 1995 look at the World Wide Web

These topics, as well as the news sources that students may have access to, have a U.S. history focus and a U.S.-centric view. There is news reporting on events and individuals from across the globe. Though that U.S.-centric view can certainly be seen in that news reporting as well, it does give students the opportunity to explore perspective and voice within the news as well as to question what U.S. news consumers were exposed to when they were creating their understanding of the world through their reading or viewing of the news.

When considering perspectives, do not discount the benefit of looking at regional perspectives within the country as national news stories are reported. Exploring regional perspectives can be a way to look at what parts of a news story are shared and emphasized by different reporters. It also encourages students to ask why news may be reported differently across the country.

Looking at regional differences in reporting is another way to incorporate news literacy into another aspect of social studies, geography. Geographic literacy, as explored earlier in this chapter, can be a deliberate means of integrating news literacy into upper elementary and middle school students' learning.

These news stories and others don't just encourage students to look at history and geography within the social studies disciplines. Connections are easily made to curricular standards related to economics and civics. Topics in these two areas have been and continue to be reported on in news. Incorporating news literacy into the teaching of economics and civics gives students authentic resources as well as meaningful examples to work from. While primary objectives may fall within these social studies disciplines, secondary objectives can target news literacy so that students can fully access and respond to the news reports being used in the lessons.

Lessons in news literacy can also be found in other areas of the humanities, specifically language arts. As students study historical fiction or nonfiction reading and writing, incorporating news on topics related to those historical topics or nonfiction topics encourages a greater depth in the context that students are exploring. This gives the opportunity for deeper understanding and greater connections in their reading or writing. It also gives an opportunity for news literacy skills to be introduced or reinforced. Realistic fiction may also invite a deep dive into current news as book titles and new reporting wrestle with social issues of the day. The incorporation of both into a student's learning can make the experience more meaningful and connected.

The reading of nonfiction is also a skill emphasized in many parts of the curriculum. Incorporating the reading of news stories into learning as a way to accomplish these learning objectives gives the opportunity to meet curricular needs and also teach important news literacy skills. Utilizing news in language arts teaching also can open up the idea of reading beyond the pages of a book. Students who may not connect with fiction stories or whose stamina may cause them to struggle with nonfiction books may find engagement and success with news text, especially when they have some choice over the news topic they are reading about.

The sciences also invite the use of news and news literacy skills. I've already written about the graphical literacy necessary to interact with some news. These direct connections to mathematics are regularly found. They, along with other data-driven news stories, can be utilized to put the concepts of mathematics in a real-world context for students to explore. Mathematical concepts can be seen through the news as a way to communicate and solve problems in ways that are not as clean and tidy as in the math book. In addition, these interactions with real-world math boost the possibility that students will do more than solve the problem. They may also come to understand that problem in a larger context and question the solution and what it means to that context. Though there may not be relevant math applications in all news literacy experiences, the ones that are there are ripe with rich learning opportunities.

The sciences are reported on heavily in the news. There may be no greater way to help upper elementary and middle school students see how the scientific process plays out in real life than to explore news reporting on scientific efforts, advancements, and discoveries. These types of reports are often much more accessible than writings that are created specifically for the scientific community. The reporting is often of high interest and, in some ways, incomplete, in that it may report on where scientists are within the process as opposed to reporting on a completed process. Targeted incorporation of scientific news connected with studied news topics gives students a connection between the learning that happens in their classroom and the rest of the world. As educators work to help students see themselves as scientists, this bridge through reported news may help accomplish that goal. Science news reports encourage students to ask questions and explore additional resources as they expand their understanding of the role the sciences play in their lives.

Another element of scientific reporting that is documented in current and historical news is that scientific understanding changes over time. Far from being a body of scientific knowledge that is set in stone as well as in the pages of books, scientific news reports, when looked at over time, show new knowledge found, mistakes made, and further understandings clarified. Carefully curated news reports on scientific topics and targeted analysis can help to illustrate this.

Let us not forget other curricular areas that may not get the spotlight but have direct connections to news literacy. Information literacy, digital literacy, and other literacies are often incorporated in similar ways as news literacy. Some of them, in your district or school, may already have made significant headway toward being integrated into students' daily learning. There is a synergistic benefit to bringing them all together as educators see the overlapping skills that make up these sets of literacies. Those overlapping skills and strategies can be intentionally pointed out to students, so that the acquisition of news literacy is built upon other literacies students have been learning. Librarians, subject-area coordinators, and others who already play a key role in incorporating these literacies into student learning may be willing partners and leaders in championing the incorporation of news literacy into existing learning. Bringing news literacy under this umbrella would expand the vision of the work done, the creativity of the learning approaches, and the resources available to students.

Offering up these opportunities for news literacy to be incorporated across subject areas in elementary and middle school settings is made easier by the structures already in place at those grade levels. In elementary schools, for example, teachers often plan across all subject areas or plan with a team if students rotate out of their home classroom for a subject or two. In many middle school settings, students have a core team of teachers who can band together for integrated learning experiences across subject areas. I'd be remiss if I didn't point directly at school librarians in both of these settings as people who have an understanding of literacies and information access that spans across grade levels, teams, and classrooms to provide a full scope of what students experience in their learning across years at a school. These elementary and middle school settings are a perfect environment for news literacy to be incorporated across subject areas to enhance student learning.

4

Lessons to Develop News Literacies

The following 21 lessons work together to give students a variety of experiences to develop news literacy. They are not meant to be taught a single time during a student's upper elementary and middle school career. These lessons should be revisited, adapted, and reshaped to accommodate students' learning needs and what other content teachers may want to include when teaching news literacy.

All lessons focus on the use of news and development of news literacy skills around a historical event or time period. With news topics ever-changing, taking the news from the months when this book was written would make a lesson instantly dated. Instead, I offer suggestions for using the same lesson approach with current news and current news delivery methods. The exit slips and organizers that accompany each lesson work equally well to teach news literacy whether students are looking at current news or news in a historical context.

The lessons have been divided up into four sections:

1. Describing the News
2. News Analysis Strategies
3. Interacting with the News
4. Understanding Oneself and Others as News Consumers

Although there is some overlap in the experiences, especially when reinforcing earlier concepts, the organization of lessons is meant to assist educators in their efforts to begin with the larger ideas of news literacy and narrow down to a specific lesson.

DESCRIBING THE NEWS

This collection of lessons focuses on giving students a foundational grounding in how to describe the news that they encounter. This includes describing content within news reports: for example, using words such as *fact* and *opinion* to describe parts of the news. It also includes describing news sources and the information they share using the terms *reliability* and *credibility*. These lessons do not provide an exhaustive list of vocabulary related to the news, but the terminology within these lessons is used in subsequent lessons later in the chapter.

Lesson 1: Fact vs. Opinion
Lesson 2: What Is News and What Isn't
Lesson 3: Differentiating Between News and News Commentary
Lesson 4: Reliability and Credibility

· Lesson 1: Fact vs. Opinion

News literacy requires a sound ability to distinguish between facts and opinions. These facts and opinions are often interwoven throughout the story, making it more of a challenge for novice news-literate readers to tell the difference between the two.

The skill is a foundational one that is built upon in later lessons. As students begin to analyze news text and audio, identifying facts and opinions will help students tell the difference between news and commentary, become aware of their own opinions as they begin to read a news story, and develop other news literacy skills.

This lesson introduces students to simple definitions for facts and opinions, asks them to apply those definitions to their own understanding of the world, and gives them practice in identifying facts and opinions when they are side-by-side in a variety of news stories.

Objectives

In this lesson, students will:

- Reinforce their understanding of a fact and an opinion.
- Predict and react to the presence of facts and opinions in news stories.
- Identify facts and opinions within print and audiovisual news stories.

A Historic Perspective

Introduce the Lesson

Begin the lesson by giving students the following definitions:

Fact: A statement that is true and can be proven
Opinion: A personal viewpoint based on one or more facts

Ask students to share examples of facts and opinions. Students can struggle with the knowledge that their personal beliefs are not, in themselves, facts. When appropriate, help students distinguish between an opinion and the fact(s) that it is based on.

If needed to describe student examples, offer two additional definitions:

Belief: An idea based on culture, morality, or value
Prejudice: An opinion based on faulty or incomplete information

The addition of definitions for beliefs and prejudice is not meant to be subsets of facts and opinions, but instead to more fully address the range of examples that students may describe that do not fall under the first two definitions.

After examples have been shared and talked through, students should have a basic understanding of facts and opinions. Tell students that news often contains both facts and opinions within the report that is shared. Note that other sources that are not news can also contain facts and opinions, but for the purposes of this lesson, focus on news reports.

Begin the Activity

Working in pairs or small groups, give each set of students a news article. Options are offered in the references for this section, but news stories used can be customized to fit a current topic of study. Stories should be short and relatively easy to comprehend. If using audiovisual news from radio, television, or newsreels, offer a transcript of the spoken words to students.

Using two different methods (for example, two different-color highlighters), ask students to identify facts and opinions within their story. As pairs or small groups finish, pair them with other students who have worked on the same article. Ask them to share their findings and come to a consensus by using the definitions at the beginning of the lesson to direct their markings.

Discussion and Ending the Activity

The larger groups should then share out to their peers. If possible, display the article of focus as the group shares a found fact and opinion within the article. Students could also be encouraged to discuss one disagreement within the group and how it was resolved.

End the lesson with the exit slip.

A Modern Perspective

Using the same activity and structure with current news will require slight modifications. It is more likely that students will be viewing or listening to news instead of reading it. Optimally, transcripts would be used, but closed captioning may also be an option. This may require students to document the facts and opinions using the provided organizer.

Any current news used should be in manageable segments and from a variety of sources, including news reported through social media.

Differentiation

Given that opinions are personal viewpoints based on facts, students can extend their understanding of facts and opinions in the news by finding the facts that support opinions. After students identify facts and opinions within a story, ask them to annotate within the article or on the organizer the fact that supports an opinion being offered.

If students are already practiced at identifying facts and opinions in other sources, challenge students in different ways with this activity. As groups of students work with different articles, ask students to identify the facts in one article. Then rotate groups so they are identifying opinions in another article. Then, in a final rotation, ask a third group to connect the work of the first two, finding facts that support opinions within the same article.

Assessment

Exit Slip		
	Opinion	*Supporting Fact*
Select an opinion from one of the news stories shared today. Identify facts that were used to support that opinion.		

REFERENCES

"Baby Is 'Shoplifter'?" *The Indianapolis Times*, 24 Dec. 1923, https://chronicling america.loc.gov/lccn/sn82015313/1923-12-24/ed-1/seq-1

"Children's Home to Get Lumber from Old Hospital Building." *The Maui News*, 13 Dec. 1921, https://chroniclingamerica.loc.gov/lccn/sn82014689/1921-12-13 /ed-1/seq-1

"Clinic Meetings Very Successful." *The Redwood Gazette*, 13 Oct. 1920, https:// chroniclingamerica.loc.gov/lccn/sn85025570/1920-10-13/ed-1/seq-1

"5,296 Children of School Age in Audrain." *Mexico Weekly Leger*, 17 Aug. 1922, https://chroniclingamerica.loc.gov/lccn/sn89067274/1922-08-17/ed-1/seq-1

Fowler, H. Ramsey. *The Little, Brown Handbook*. Little, Brown, 1980.

"Grammar School Feeds 360 Children." *Daily Picayune*, 4 Mar. 1921, https:// chroniclingamerica.loc.gov/lccn/sn89051256/1921-03-04/ed-1/seq-1

Organizer

Fact and Opinion in News	
News story topic or title	
circle one	List facts and opinions from the news story. Quote the news story exactly.
Fact / Opinion	
Fact / Opinion	
Fact / Opinion	
Fact / Opinion	
Fact / Opinion	
Fact / Opinion	
Fact / Opinion	
Fact / Opinion	

Lesson 2: What Is News and What Isn't

Students today receive a lot of news; more than that, they receive a lot of information. That information can look like news. If news is elevated and has the prestige of being less subjective, there may be confusion if subjective information is believed to be news. How are students supposed to tell the difference between news and non-news information?

This lesson aims to give students experience identifying news and non-news items. Given a simple definition, students can identify a news story and describe why it is news. This lesson depends on students having an understanding of the difference between fact and opinion. Lesson one helps to set that foundation. This lesson also begins to lay the groundwork for a future lesson on the reliability and credibility of news sources.

Objectives

In this lesson, students will:

- Understand a simple definition of news.
- Identify communications that are similar to news.
- Describe why a broadcast or published item is news.
- Sort information given in public venues dependent upon whether it fits a definition for news.

A Historic Perspective

Introduce the Lesson

Give students the assigned newspaper or section of a newspaper. One possibility is suggested in the reference list at the end of this lesson. Share that newspapers may not be defined as expected because they do not only contain news.

Begin the Activity

Ask students how they would define *news*. Record their definitions for later review. Give students a definition and ask them to use it for the remainder of the lesson: *News—A broadcast or publication to inform about a recent event.*

Ask students to identify key elements in the definition that could help us identify a piece of information as "news." Look for students to identify that news is "broadcast or published" to show how it is disseminated, that it is meant "to inform" to demonstrate its purpose, and that it concerns "recent events" connecting it to a moment in time.

Once all three areas are identified, brainstorm with students about types of communication that are examples of non-news because they do not meet all three criteria. A straightforward example would be an advertisement that is broadcast or published and may be connected to events of the day but has the intention of informing about a product and making it appealing to the viewer of the advertisement.

Give pairs of students the published page listed in the reference section of this lesson. For each part of the newspaper page, students can use the graphic organizer to document their understanding of whether the item is news or not. As pairs of students work through items, return to a class discussion periodically to discuss items that may be confusing to the students. Using the definition, determine whether it should be described as news.

Discussion and Ending the Activity

Revisit students' earlier definitions for *news*. Ask how they react to those definitions after the lesson. Would a student like to make changes to a previously suggested definition? Is there an element in a student's definition that should be considered for the class definition?

A Modern Perspective

Using the same structure, provide students with news and other information that is shared widely today. Include social media posts, articles, and advertisements from aggregated news feeds, and online video.

Encourage the challenging discussions of whether something shared on social media is "published or broadcast." Another example could include a shared news story from a local newspaper or television station that also includes an opinion from the person who shared the story. Ask students if this opinion should be considered news. The discussion should come back to the definition of news and viewing shared information through that lens.

Differentiation

- Use a newspaper that reports on a topic of choice or is from a time period of study.
- Use a variety of information sources for students' determinations of news or not-news.
- If time does not allow, do not ask students their definitions of news. Simply offer your definition.
- Extend the assignment by asking students to listen, watch, and read information throughout the week to gather additional examples of news and not-news.

Assessment

Exit Slip	
When looking at information that someone has shared with you, how can you tell if it should be described as "news"?	

REFERENCE

National Endowment for the Humanities. "Harrisburg Telegraph (Harrisburg, Pa.) 1879–1948, March 13, 1919, Page 6." *Chronicling America*, chroniclingamerica .loc.gov/lccn/sn85038411/1919-03-13/ed-1/seq-6

Organizer

Definition of *News*: A broadcast or publication to inform about a recent event.				
Item (*briefly describe the source*)	Is the source broadcast or published?	Is the source meant to inform?	Is the source about a recent event (compared to when it was created)?	Does the source meet all three criteria to be described as news?

Lesson 3: Differentiating Between News and News Commentary

There has been a blurring of the lines between news and news commentary. The common element is the means of delivery and is seen mostly in broadcast news. It is not unusual for news anchors and hosts to both report the news and comment on it. For those developing news literacy skills, one individual playing both those roles can make it difficult to understand what is news and what is not. This does not even take into account programming, most often political and in soft news formats, that can best be described as news entertainment.

There are formal journalistic definitions for news, commentaries, and editorials. For the purpose of news literacy learning, we are not concerned about these defined types of news. Instead, students will focus on different types of content within the news and the interplay among them.

Students developing news literacy need to learn to deal with the news they have access to and make meaning from the information it shares. The lesson on facts and opinions or other experiences that provide students a sound understanding of facts and opinions is an important element for students to bring into this lesson.

In this lesson, students use news resources focused on the 1963 Birmingham campaign from another lesson, "Interacting with and Reacting to Emotionally Charged News Topics" (Lesson 20). These lessons could be combined or different news resources could be used. Here, students look at two news resources: one that is information focused, and another that is opinion focused.

Objectives

In this lesson, students will:

- Identify facts and opinions in two related published articles.
- Determine the purpose of each article for the audience.
- Given a definition for *news commentary*, discuss the difference between that and news reporting in different formats.

A Historic Perspective

Introduce the Lesson

Revisit the definition of news: *News is a broadcast or published report to inform about recent events.* Begin by asking students if there are other forms of media that inform them but also do something else in addition to informing them. Students may recognize other forms of media that do this. If not, offer advertising as a form of media that is meant to inform people and entice them to purchase something. Make note, with students, of whether any of their other forms of media involve news-related material or recent events.

Tell students that there are other types of media that can contain news elements. To discover them, it is important to identify what they try to do. Share examples again of advertisements having the effect of enticing people to buy something and news having the effect of people becoming informed. Note that one is not better than another. They simply serve different purposes.

Begin the Activity

Inform students that they will look at two sources today, both on the same topic. With both sources, students will be asked to watch and read through a lens of opinions and facts. Begin by sharing the news article from the *Jackson Advocate* from May 11, 1963, "Early Efforts of Justice Dept. Rep. Fails to Produce Compromise." Ask students, using the organizer, to identify passages from the report that resonated with them or that they feel are important to the understanding of the article. For each of the passages, students should select an accompanying label, "opinion" or "fact."

Invite students to share their statements from the news broadcast and related labels. Discuss any disagreements as to whether a statement should be labeled a fact or an opinion.

Provide students with the article "The Shame of Birmingham" from the May 10, 1963, *Arizona Tribune.* Ask students to do the same analysis. Students may use the organizer or they may annotate directly onto a print or digital copy of the article. Students should continue by sharing their findings with the class and come to a consensus on any disagreements about the labeling of fact or opinion.

In small groups, ask students to return to both articles and identify how each is meant to affect the people who watch or read the pieces. If helpful, remind them of the earlier examples and encourage students to focus on their passages and labels from earlier in the lesson. After students have connected each source to an intent for the audience, discuss the thoughts of each group. Look for common audience intent as well as support for their reasoning from examples in the articles.

Discussion and Ending the Activity

Present a new word and definition to students. *Commentary: Opinions or explanations related to an event.* Put this new definition alongside the definition of *news.* Ask students if they can create a definition for a new term: *news commentary.* Look for students to incorporate the word "recent" into the definition of the word "commentary." Students may also incorporate the phrase "published or broadcast" to show how news commentary is shared.

End the lesson with the exit slip.

A Modern Perspective

Some modern news reporting has a noticeable amount of commentary. Using video editing software, students can edit a report to remove all commentary.

Ask students to compare the original and edited reports. Look at how viewers may be affected by or receive each report.

Extend the activity using modern news by asking students to find examples of news commentary utilizing their created definition. Students should use formats and sources of news that they may already encounter. Encourage students to include examples of what was shared in the source to support its labeling as news commentary.

Differentiation

If using broadcast news, to process news reports more rapidly, students may work in pairs to identify as many quoted passages from the report as possible. If needed, student pairs can continue to confer with each other on labeling passages as opinion or fact.

When film and written news and commentary are available in abundance with historical or current news, consider comparing the two formats. Ask students to determine what format may be more likely to provide more factually based reporting based on a limited examination of the available examples.

Assessment

Exit Slip	
What are the benefits of knowing whether the news program you watch, listen to, or read is news reporting or news commentary?	

REFERENCES

"Early Efforts of Justice Dept. Rep. Fails to Produce Compromise." *Jackson Advocate*, 11 May 1963, https://chroniclingamerica.loc.gov/lccn/sn79000083/1963-05-11/ed-1/seq-1

"The Shame of Birmingham." *Arizona Tribune*, 10 May 1963, https://chroniclingamerica.loc.gov/lccn/sn84021918/1963-05-10/ed-1/seq-1

Organizer

<table>
<tr><td colspan="2">Source#1</td></tr>
<tr><td>Quote from Source</td><td>Opinion or Fact</td></tr>
<tr><td></td><td></td></tr>
<tr><td></td><td></td></tr>
<tr><td></td><td></td></tr>
<tr><td></td><td></td></tr>
<tr><td></td><td></td></tr>
<tr><td colspan="2">Does this source contain a larger number of facts or opinions?

</td></tr>
<tr><td colspan="2">How is this source meant to affect those who interact with it? How do you know?

</td></tr>
</table>

<table>
<tr><td colspan="2">Source #2</td></tr>
<tr><td>Quote from Source</td><td>Opinion or Fact</td></tr>
<tr><td></td><td></td></tr>
<tr><td></td><td></td></tr>
<tr><td></td><td></td></tr>
<tr><td></td><td></td></tr>
<tr><td></td><td></td></tr>
<tr><td colspan="2">Does this source contain a larger number of facts or opinions?

</td></tr>
<tr><td colspan="2">How is this source meant to affect those who interact with it? How do you know?

</td></tr>
</table>

Lesson 4: Reliability and Credibility

As people read, watch, and listen to news, there should be two regular questions they ask themselves: Do I trust this source of news? and Is this news information believable? These, at their foundation, are the questions behind reliable news sources and credible information. These two words, *reliability* and *credibility*, are often used interchangeably. However, as the lesson shows, reliability is a measure of the trustworthiness of the source, whereas credibility is a measure of the believability of the information.

What can become tricky for students is that these measures change over time and are dependent on each other. As students become better informed about a news topic, information that initially seemed more credible may be found less so. The news source where that information came from may then become less reliable in their eyes.

This idea that more news sources can change students' perception of reliability of sources and credibility of information connects with a lesson later in the book on corroboration (Lesson 14). Although these ideas are intrinsically tied together, the lessons themselves are broken up to make them more manageable for teaching and learning. This lesson focuses on a source unknown to students publishing a news story about the sinking of the *Titanic* on April 15, 1912. The news report contains misinformation that many students will be able to identify as not credible.

Objectives

In this lesson, students will:

- Investigate a news source to find background information.
- Read a news story through a lens of credibility.
- Make an initial determination of reliability of a source and credibility of information.
- Give evidence from findings to explain why a source is more or less reliable and information is more or less credible.

A Historic Perspective

Introduce the Lesson

Begin by introducing students to the terms *reliable* and *credible* in relation to reading, watching, or listening to the news.

Tell students that *reliability* refers to the person or institution reporting the news. Another word for reliable could be "trustworthy." Ask students, "Why would it be important for a news source to be reliable or trustworthy?" Look for student responses comparing a trustworthy source to the quality of information coming from that source. Then introduce *credibility* as a term connected to the information that a source shares along with a synonym for credibility, *believability.*

Ask students, after first requesting them not to share any stories or names, if they have ever thought that someone was extremely reliable. Look for evidence that what that person said or did could be trusted. Next, ask students if they have ever heard of someone who didn't seem credible or believable. Point out that these two terms can be used regarding sources of news and the information those sources share.

Begin the Activity

Share the header of the front page of *The Day Book* from April 15, 1912. Ask students if they know anything about this publication. It is likely that students will not, although some may notice the location where the newspaper was printed (Chicago), and the date of publication. Ask students what they know about the source's reliability or trustworthiness. At best, students may infer that because it is a newspaper publication, it may be trustworthy.

Acknowledge that if you know nothing about the source, it is difficult to determine how reliable that source is. Ask:

- How could we find out if this newspaper is trustworthy or reliable?
- How might reading the news articles in the newspaper help us determine whether it is reliable?

Reveal the rest of the front page of the newspaper. Ask students to share their initial ideas about the reliability of the source as well as the credibility of the information using the organizer. Remind students, as they read the article, to read through a lens of looking for evidence of credibility or believability.

Discussion and Ending the Activity

Ask students to share their findings and thoughts about the credibility of the information found in the newspaper. As students cite background information as a driving force in determining the credibility of information, ask:

- What would you do if you didn't have background knowledge about the news event? How could you determine the credibility of a single news report?
- If there is specific information in the news report that you do not believe is credible, what does that make you think about the information in the same news story that you are not sure about?

End the lesson with the exit slip.

A Modern Perspective

If students have little or no background knowledge or knowledge of a source, it is difficult for them to determine reliability and credibility. Consider using an article from a tabloid newspaper or tabloid online resource. Utilizing Wikipedia or another encyclopedia source may help students determine reliability prior to reading or interacting with the article.

Some news stories from tabloid sources may contain disinformation that students believe to be true. Consider returning to definitions from Lesson 1 for facts, opinions, beliefs, and prejudices to ground the conversation. Ask students which of these would be most important to consider when determining believability. If not all students agree that facts are the most important factor, come to an agreement by consensus.

Differentiation

To extend students' understanding of the reliability of the source, share the source page for *The Day Book* that gives information about the newspaper's publication. Ask students to use that background to determine the reliability of the source.

Using this news topic or another where initial reporting may be flawed, ask students to search Chronicling America or another newspaper database for reports across multiple newspapers from the same day. Challenge students to determine the credibility of information based on their background knowledge and evolving understanding of the news event.

Assessment

Exit Slip	
If you continue to learn more about a news story, you will read, watch, and listen to more news. How might the reliability of early sources and the credibility of early information change as you learn more? Why does that happen?	

REFERENCES

"Chronicling America Advanced Search." *Chronicling America: Library of Congress*, chroniclingamerica.loc.gov/#tab=tab_advanced_search

"The Day Book. [Volume]." *News about Chronicling America RSS*, chronicling america.loc.gov/lccn/sn83045487

"The Day Book. [Volume] (Chicago, Ill.) 1911–1917, April 15, 1912, Image 1." *News about Chronicling America RSS*, chroniclingamerica.loc.gov/lccn/sn83045487 /1912-04-15/ed-1/seq-1

Organizer

Source:	
What do you know about this source?	
How trustworthy or reliable do you feel the source is?	
What evidence about the source informs you about its reliability?	
What is the focus of this news story? What do you know about the topic?	
After you read, watch, or listen to the news, how believable or credible do you think it is?	
What evidence from the news story informs you about its credibility?	

NEWS ANALYSIS STRATEGIES

The lessons in this series give students a toolkit of strategies to analyze the news that they read, watch, and listen to. These analysis strategies can be used together or separately as students engage with the news. In different ways, each strategy helps students engage with news reporting in deeper ways to establish an understanding of the topic being reported. They are all based on analysis strategies used to develop historical thinking skills.

Lesson 5: Sourcing: Taking a First Look at New Information
Lesson 6: Contextualizing: Placing News in the Moment
Lesson 7: Close Reading: Uncovering the Story
Lesson 8: Corroborating Information Across Multiple Sources
Lesson 9: Asking Questions When Interacting with News
Lesson 10: Word Choice in the News
Lesson 11: Voices in the News: Finding Who Is Heard and Who Is Not

Lesson 5: Sourcing: Taking a First Look at New Information

Sourcing is a quick process where readers and viewers can focus on the source of the story, both the individual who wrote it and the organization that published it. They can use that information to understand the story more completely. Sourcing may even encourage readers and viewers not to interact with the story if they find the source to be unreliable. In addition to looking at the source of the news article, students briefly browse the news article to identify the topic. This information is used for another strategy, contextualizing the news source.

Inspired by the Stanford History Education Group's Reading Like a Historian process, students in this lesson are asked to source several news stories in different formats. The process of sourcing a piece of information does not have to be exclusive to news stories. In this lesson, students will go through the basic steps of sourcing a news article. Timing will be key, as they will require slightly more time to do this task if they have never sourced an article before. This will still only take minutes, though. As students become more adept at sourcing, it can take them less than a minute to source a news article.

Objectives

In this lesson, students will:

- Interact with news stories to examine the source of the news stories.
- Identify what they do not know about the source of a news story.
- Search for additional information beyond the story to understand the source.
- Determine whether the source of a news story makes it a reliable source for news.

A Historical Perspective

Introduce the Lesson

Introduce sourcing as a strategy to briefly look at the individual who created or organization that published a piece of news. Ask students why knowing the source of news might be important. Look for answers that reference the perspective of the person or group reporting the news as well as the reliability of the information.

Begin the Activity

Give students the graphic organizer and link to the article "Jim Crow Bus Boycott Hits Co. Pocketbook."

Tell students that sourcing news should be able to be done quickly without reading, viewing, or listening to the entire story. Encourage them to skim print and any additional information given to answer the first row of questions on the organizer. Give them one and a half to two minutes to do this. Ask students to share responses to gain a collective understanding of the limited information that is gained when sourcing an article.

Ask students about the second row of questions. How might they answer those questions? If not offered as responses, offer that links on the page or quick web searches may provide information. Remind students that this should also be a quick process. Give students three to five minutes to find additional information and record their findings.

In pairs or small groups, ask students to discuss what they know about this news story before reading the full story.

- How can they know the topic of the story without reading the entire article?
- How does sourcing a news story help inform the reader?
- Is it important to know where news comes from? Why?

Discussion and Ending the Activity

After students have an opportunity to develop their ideas in the smaller groups, extend the discussion to the whole class.

End the lesson with the exit slip.

A Modern Perspective

Repeat this activity with a current news story from a national news source or a news service that the elementary or middle school subscribes to.

An added element of sourcing in modern-day news stories is news being shared through social networking platforms. If a number of students use social networking platforms, ask if anyone in their network has shared news online. Include the person who shared the news, the messenger, in sourcing the news article.

Explain that while a person who shares a news story over an online social network is not the creator or publisher of the news, they are part of the sourcing because they have shared it with others. Ask, "How might knowing why this person shared a news story help us understand more about it even before we read it?" Encourage students to share personal examples without revealing the names of those who are sharing news stories.

Differentiation

- Ask students to source different formats of news stories.
- Identify a historical news story directly connected to curricular content.

- Source a current local news story.
- Use a current news story shared by your district, building, or other professional online social networking account.

Assessment

Exit Slip	
How can learning about the source of a news story help inform you before you read, watch, or listen to it?	

REFERENCE

Gitano, H. "Jim Crow Bus Boycott Hits Co. Pocketbook." *Arizona Sun*, 20 Jan. 1956, p. 4, https://chroniclingamerica.loc.gov/lccn/sn84021917/1956-01-20/ed-1 /seq-4

Organizer

Sourcing for Historical News				
News Source	What format is the story? (print, video, audio)	Who created the story?	What company or organization published the story?	When was the story created?
You may have to do a quick search or scan to answer these questions.	What do you know about the person who created the story or the organization that published it?		Without reading or listening to the full news story, determine the topic being reported.	

Sourcing for Current News				
News Source	What format is the story? (print, video, audio)	Who created the story?	What company or organization published the story?	When was the story created?
You may have to do a quick search or scan to answer these questions.	What do you know about the person who created the story or the organization that published it?		What do you know about the person or group that shared the story?	
Without reading or listening to the full news story, determine the topic being reported.				

Lesson 6: Contextualizing: Placing News in the Moment

We often click on or watch news stories that we have some contextual knowledge of. Taking the time to bring any personal knowledge of a news story to the forefront prior to reading or viewing it gives students an opportunity to exercise other skills to follow, such as checks on the news article's perspective and accuracy. The credibility of information and reliability of the source can also be influenced by the contextual knowledge that news consumers bring to news reports. Contextualizing a news topic also encourages students to check for new understanding and ask questions after interacting with the article.

In this lesson, students are given some contextual knowledge of an event and then a related news article. They use that contextual knowledge to place the news story in the larger context of the event.

Objectives

In this lesson, students will:

- Identify a news topic through minimal interaction with a news story.
- Reflect on their own understanding around the topic of a news story.
- React to a news story given their previous understanding of the topic.

A Historic Perspective

Introduce the Lesson

To give students context of an event, read them the picture book *Around America to Win the Vote* by Mara Rockliff and Hadley Hooper. If possible, do this prior to the rest of the lesson (up to two weeks prior) to give students an opportunity to draw upon their memory of the events recounted in the book.

Begin the Activity

Begin the second phase of the lesson by sharing that a news story is always part of a bigger event or topic. A short video or article can only tell so much of a larger event. Tell students that they will be reading a news story, but that to understand the story they will have to put it in context.

Give students the topic of Alice Burke's and Nell Richardson's trip across the United States in 1916. Ask students to take three to five minutes to write about what they know about that event using the organizer. Encourage them to include questions as evidence of what they do not know about the event and information about related events connected to this topic. Have a short whole-class conversation after students write to share context, questions, and related information.

Give students the news article, "The Golden Flier Enroute to Phoenix," from the May 14, 1916 issue of the *Arizona Republican*. Ask students to read the article. Invite them to read through the lens of the context, questions, and related information that they just wrote down. Encourage them to annotate the article while reading.

In small-group discussions, ask students to react to the article, sharing what they now know about the trip and how it connects to what they previously knew or questioned.

Discussion and Ending the Activity

Ask students to revisit the organizer to document new understanding and questions. Point out that even though a news article is meant to inform the reader, it can cause us to ask questions and search for the answers in other news articles or other sources.

End the lesson with the exit slip.

A Modern Perspective

Although many students may have more context related to news stories from today, it is likely that not all students will have contextual knowledge. Providing that contextual knowledge through whole-class conversations can give the teacher an understanding of what students know about a topic in the news, as well as reveal and share a general understanding amongst the class members.

Current topics and news stories may cause stronger emotional reactions from students than historical news. Pair lessons on contextualization with students' identification of their own perspectives on topics of news stories. This combination of skills can have a positive impact on how they interact with the news story.

Share with students that contextualizing a topic for a news article does not always mean writing down information. People may do this internally as they begin to interact with the news and may even use their contextual knowledge to decide whether they will read or watch a particular news article.

Differentiation

- Students can contextualize in a short video or through drawing images. Part of the reflection on the topic can also be done in a small-group discussion, but provide every student with some quiet time to reflect on the topic before beginning a discussion.
- In modern or historical interactions, allow students to view a series of headlines as they contextualize the news story. Ask students to choose among those headlines to determine which news story they will interact with.

- After contextualizing, give students different news stories on the same topic. Following their reading of the news stories, ask them to reflect on their new context in small groups or a whole-class discussion.

Assessment

Exit Slip	
How does reflecting on the topic of a news story before reading it affect your reading of the news story?	

REFERENCE

"The Golden Flier Enroute to Phoenix." *Arizona Republican*, 14 May 1916, https:// chroniclingamerica.loc.gov/lccn/sn84020558/1916-05-14/ed-1/seq-15

Organizer

News Topic:		
News Story Title:		
Context	**Questions**	**Related Information**

After interacting with the news story, what new context, questions, and related information to the topic do you have?

Context	**Questions**	**Related Information**

Lesson 7: Close Reading: Uncovering the Story

At the heart of interacting with a news story—whether a student is reading, watching, or listening—is to have a way to analyze or process the information. For many lessons in this book, I suggest that students use a close reading strategy. There are other ways to analyze text. I use this method with my students because it is simple and easy to remember. Our analysis process is inspired by the book *Falling in Love with Close Reading* by Christopher Lehman and Kate Roberts.

The close reading strategy has three steps. They are not always all used, depending on the intended learning. In the first step of the process, the students read (or watch or listen) to a news story through a specific lens. Examples may be to look for basic comprehension, to identify persons involved in the news story, or to identify the audience that would be affected by the news story. The second step is for students to review the information they have gathered and look for patterns. Often I ask them to group the identified information from the first step and name the groups. In the final step, students use their findings from the first two steps to summarize the information. With news stories, examples might be to write a headline, rewrite part of the story, or write a letter to the editor on the news topic.

In this lesson, students will perform a close reading analysis of a televised news story from the 1995 North Carolina State Fair. The interesting factor in the story is the reporting on the World Wide Web. Students will focus on making connections to the technology of today. In this lesson, students will have a transcript of the report available. This will give them options to access the information from the story or reference it in print as they analyze.

Objectives

In this lesson, students will:

- Perform a close reading analysis of a news story.
- Read through multiple lenses to understand a news story.
- Summarize a news story focusing on its purpose and significance.

A Historic Perspective

Introduce the Lesson

Begin by asking students how they make sense of information when they read, watch, or listen to news reports. Many may share that they simply read, watch, or listen. Others may point to certain strategies such as reading headlines or captions.

Share with students that they will be learning to use a close reading strategy that can be used to focus on news stories or almost any writing. Also, explain that the strategy has only three steps, so it is easy to remember, but the steps may be slightly different each time so that the strategy can be used with different types of sources.

Explain step one as "reading through a lens." Compare it to reading with a very specific purpose. Give an example such as reading a recipe while focusing on ingredients. Why might people do that? Possibly to make sure they have all of the ingredients or to prepare for a trip to the store. Similarly, "reading through a lens" is reading with a very intentional purpose that will prepare us for steps two and three.

Begin the Activity

Give students the organizer and tell them that they will be viewing and listening to the news report through the lens of "understanding technology" reported on in the story. Direct students to the October 18, 1995, episode segment of North Carolina Now. Provide students with a transcript of the news report if they would like one. (The transcript for this lesson can be copied from the website given in the reference section.) Tell students that they should be jotting notes as they listen to and watch the report. They will be able to watch it more than once. Encourage students to quote directly from the episode and give short written descriptions of what they see.

After students have watched the segment two to three times and gathered their information, ask students to briefly share with a partner. Encourage them to add information from their discussion to their own organizer if they would like.

Moving on to step two, tell students that they will take their current list of quotes and descriptions from step one and organize those items into groups. Tell students that:

- Not all information has to be placed in a group.
- A piece of information can be used in more than one group.
- Groups can have different numbers of items in them.
- There is not a set number of groups.
- There is not a specific way the items have to be grouped.

Ask students to continue with step two with a partner. If both partners have a similar quote or description, they can combine it or use just one of them as they are grouping items. As partners begin forming groups, ask them to give the groups they created categories or titles to show others why the items were grouped together. As partners finish step two, ask for volunteers to share some of the categories they created with their grouped items.

Tell students that they will use their work from the first two steps to complete step three, where they will demonstrate their new understanding. In this case, they will do a quick write independently. Give students the following prompt for their quick write:

Using your understanding from the news report, if a person traveled back in time to 1995, what might their interactions with technology be and how would they be different from what they are used to?

Discussion and Ending the Activity

Give students three to five minutes for the quick write. If time allows, ask students to share with their partner or with the class as a whole.

Close the class with the exit slip.

A Modern Perspective

Current newscasts, if using televised news or video reports online, should have a closed captioning option. This can give students an instant transcript. With them viewing a visual news story, running captions, and listening, it is likely that they will need to take in the story once before they begin documenting their first step in the process. Still, provide the lens for viewing the story before they interact with it for the first time.

With shorter descriptions of news stories through headlines, running news tickers at the bottoms of screens, short social media blurbs that link to longer stories, and other similar resources, students can do a variation of this activity beginning with only those short news clippings. Have students view, read, and listen to these as their step one, giving them a lens as they would normally have. Continue with step two as normal. Step three can be a form of synthesizing the information across multiple sources, including an opportunity to ask questions based on information they do not have. After students have had an introduction to the news topic through the analysis, have them interact with a full news report on the same topic.

Differentiation

If a news story contains unknown vocabulary, consider providing a glossary for students. Students who are more advanced in the analysis process may be able to identify unknown vocabulary and find definitions independently.

Use a different format of a news story to vary how students interact with the news during the analysis process. Print or audio news reports may prompt students to analyze the news in different ways. For audio news stories, accommodations may have to be made by providing students with transcripts.

There are advantages to incorporating different levels of collaboration at any time during a news story analysis. Vary the amount of collaboration among individual work, pair work, small-group work, and whole-class work based on the needs of your students and the learning environment that already exists.

Give students multiple options for sharing their new understanding. A grid of options may give them some guidance on how they decide to share their new learning.

The end of the 1995 news segment has a graph that illustrates attendance at the fair. Extend the lesson with a lesson on graphical literacy where students predict future attendance at the fair based on previous attendance. If weather data from those 1995 dates can be accessed, students can use that to further inform their predictions.

Assessment

Exit Slip	
Is reading through a lens different for you than simply reading? If so, how?	

REFERENCES

Lehman, Christopher, and Kate Roberts. *Falling in Love with Close Reading: Lessons for Analyzing Texts—and Life.* Heinemann, 2014.

"North Carolina Now; North Carolina Now Episode from 10/18/1995." UNC-TV, American Archive of Public Broadcasting (WGBH and the Library of Congress), Boston, MA and Washington, DC. 25 May 2020. https://american archive.org/catalog/cpb-aacip-129-48ffbqzc?start=38.3&end=328.45

News Topic:
News Source:
Step 1: Read through a lens:
Step 2: Look for patterns. Using the individual words or short phrases you wrote, find a way to put them into multiple groups.
Step 3: Show your new understanding.

Lesson 8: Corroborating Information Across Multiple Sources

When I speak with my students about news literacy, one element that almost always surfaces is corroborating a news story across multiple sources. It is also one skill that is at risk of not being developed with other news literacy skills. Why? Because it takes enough additional time that it can be an unappealing option. Often, if working with news reports in class, time is at a premium. Teachers, therefore, may eliminate it altogether or make it a task that students are asked to do outside of class.

It is important, though. It can weed out misinformation in the news as well as disinformation presenting itself as news. More often, it can broaden the news topic for the novice news consumer. Corroborating can open a person up to different perspectives, additional information, and other voices surrounding one news topic. It is a practice that can make a person well informed about the news of the day.

When is it most important to do this if limited by time or other elements? Possibly when students feel the strongest connection to a news story. When the topic, language, tone, or visuals of a news story elicit a strong emotional reaction of any sort, a first instinct can be to share it or dismiss it immediately. Pushing back against that instinct and instead reading across multiple news stories can benefit the news consumer.

This lesson focuses on corroborating information across a single news topic at a single moment. Other lessons show this news analysis strategy used in different contexts. Students will begin with one article on the bombing of Pearl Harbor. They will work to corroborate the information from the article while also identifying new information across additional articles.

Objectives

In this lesson, students will:

- Contextualize the content of a news article using prior knowledge.
- Identify key pieces of information within a news article.
- Corroborate information in one news article across multiple news articles.
- Recognize new information in subsequent news stories.

A Historic Perspective

Introduce the Lesson

Begin the lesson by asking students if they ever read, watch, or listen to multiple reports on the same event, topic, or person. Students may share watching guides on a new video game or view multiple trailers for the same movie. Ask students why they do this. Students may respond that these sources all deal with something that they are interested in, excited for, or want to know more about. Share with students that the same is true of news reports.

Select articles on the December 7th, 1941 bombing of Pearl Harbor by doing an advanced search in Chronicling America or another historical news database. In Chronicling America, restrict the search date to December 8th, 1941, and the search term to "Pearl Harbor."

Begin the Activity

Begin by asking students to record in the organizer what they already know about Pearl Harbor. Share with students that responses can be as broad as it being a place in the United States or as specific as details about the importance of that place in history. This is simply meant to activate students' thinking about the news topic. There is no need for students to share their thoughts or to give students additional resources if they lack contextual knowledge on the subject.

Next, give all students the same selected article on the bombing of Pearl Harbor. Ask students to analyze the article using a close reading strategy, looking through the lens of information gathering. Students can write words or short phrases from the article in the organizer or annotate them directly on the article. Check in with the class to see what information from the article was identified by the students.

Ask students to do this with two more articles. These can be the same articles for each student or can be various articles from the search results. Using varied articles may be beneficial if some students would be more successful with shorter or longer articles on the topic.

After students have read three articles, inform students that they will be moving to the next step of the analysis, corroborating information. Briefly return to the conversation at the beginning of the lesson about why students interact with multiple pieces of information on the same topic. Share that corroborating information is a way to look across multiple sources to see what information is present in more than one news report.

Ask students to return to the organizer or articles where they have the findings from their close reading analysis. Working in pairs, students should identify information that is in more than one article. They should also identify unique information that is in only one source. Students should not revisit the entire article to do this, but instead use only the information that they identified through their close reading.

Discussion and Ending the Activity

Ask students:

• What should we think about the information that was found in all three articles?

- What should we think about information that was found in just one article?
- If we read multiple articles on one topic and one article had very little or no information that matched up with the others, what should we think of that article? What if that one article was the only article we read?

After the discussion, end the lesson with the exit slip.

A Modern Perspective

Although news reports in an initial lesson on corroborating information should typically be from the same day, consider utilizing multiple formats of news sharing to gather and compare information. Televised news, printed news, online news, and news from reputable sources on social media can all be used. The analysis of each source may be slightly different, but keep the focus on the information that comes from each source.

News aggregators can be a valuable tool for finding multiple stories on one news topic from a variety of sources. Most will likely be written stories, but the items available may also contain embedded sources of video and sometimes social media. These aggregators regularly change results, so if students are using the aggregators, their results may vary over hours and days. Use methods already in place for your class or school for documenting and saving links to online sources for students to return to the news reports if they will be used across multiple days or lessons.

Differentiation

Students may perform their own searches on Chronicling America or another historical news database to find articles from different sources on the same topic. Teach students to use advanced search features to limit results to one day of reporting. Remember that news reporting was slower in the past. The preferred day to search for news articles may not be the day after an event but several days after an event, depending on the significance of the event and when in history it took place. Do several test searches to find the best results.

Assessment

Exit Slip
What are some possible benefits and drawbacks of reading, listening to, or watching multiple news reports on the same topic?	

REFERENCE

National Endowment for the Humanities. "Chronicling America Advanced Search." *Chronicling America: Library of Congress*, chroniclingamerica.loc.gov/#tab =tab_advanced_search

Organizer

News Topic and Date:
Contextualize: What do you know about this topic?
Source 1:
Close Reading for Information about the News Topic:
Source 2:
Close Reading for Information about the News Topic:
Source 3:
Close Reading for Information about the News Topic:
Highlight in one color information that is found in more than one source. Use a second color to highlight information that is found in only one source.

Lesson 9: Asking Questions When Interacting with News

News is not meant to only inform us. It should also encourage us to ask questions that we can seek to answer with additional news reporting. When news is reporting a story at the moment with limited print space or air time, part of the story is often left unsaid. Perspectives can be ignored by one news source. We, as news consumers, may not have the full context. It is important then to look for those gaps in our understanding as well as gaps in the reporting itself. Students, as they become news literate, should make it an ongoing practice to ask questions as they interact with news.

Context becomes a key factor in asking questions when interacting with news. If students are not familiar with contextualizing a news story, they should experience that lesson first.

In this historical lesson, students are given a short news report about the end of ballooning as a form of surveillance in the U.S. Civil War. Given students' likely understanding and the reporting itself, there will be a lack of context that will give an opportunity to ask questions. This cycle of questioning, as students learn more through consuming more news, will take place as a whole class to mimic what may be seen through the use of social media. Adaptations with current news can take advantage of this same strategy.

Objectives

In this lesson, students will:

- Interact with a short news story and identify the context they are lacking.
- Ask questions based on the given information and personal context of an event.
- Seek out answers to questions through additional news stories.
- Identify questions answered while asking new questions when reading a news story.

A Historic Perspective

Introduce the Lesson

Begin by asking students why people interact with news stories, whether they read, watch, or listen to the news. At least one student will likely share that the purpose is to get information. If not offered as a response, share with students that another reason to read, watch, or listen to news is to ask questions.

Begin the Activity

Tell students that they will be asking questions as part of their reading of the news from the Civil War. Offer students the short article titled "The End of Ballooning in the Army." Ask students to read the article twice. In their first read, ask them to read through a lens of understanding the big idea of the article.

As a class, identify the topic of the news story. Possible topics could be "military using balloons to observe," "the Army using balloons in the Civil War," or "the end of balloons used in the Army." Using the organizer, students should document anything they already know about the topic. Remind students they do not need to know about the entire topic to write what they know. For example, if the term *Civil War* is part of the topic, they could share something they know about the Civil War. If they know something about ballooning but not during the time of the Civil War, they could share that information. Give students two to three minutes to write down their own connections. Ask for volunteers to share. Document their sharing for a collective knowledge that students can draw from.

For the second reading of the article, ask students to read through the lens of questioning. Ask students, as they read, to write as many questions as they can about the topic of the news article. Encourage them to use information from the article to frame their questions. Give students four to five minutes to read and write questions. Then ask them to share questions and collect them.

Ask students what would be the next logical step after asking questions. Likely, someone will share the option of finding answers. Offer the possibility that other news stories may contain some of their answers. Point students toward the Civil War Ballooning Recommended Topics page in Chronicling America. Point out the selected articles, noting that the article that the students already read was the last in the list.

Be sure the previous list of student-generated questions is visible in the learning area or available digitally for all students. Briefly review the questions. Tell students that the next step is to read more widely. Allow students to select articles, or assign articles to individuals or pairs of students. Ask them to read with the purpose of answering previous questions but also asking new questions.

Ask students to focus on finding answers to their own questions but to look for information to answer others' questions as well. As students find new information in the set of news articles, invite them to share the information collectively. If working on boards or chart paper, students may use sticky notes to add answers or partial answers to questions. If working digitally, a shared document can collect information from multiple students at once. As students share any information, ask them to give some agreed-upon identification to show the article that it came from.

Students are also tasked with asking new questions. Ask students to read each article a second time with the purpose of asking new questions. New organizers may be used for students to jot down questions. Questions may also be shared with the group as a whole.

Discussion and Ending the Activity

After allowing a reasonable amount of time for students to read at least one to two new articles, answer questions, and form new questions, bring the class together to review newly shared information. Ask students to compare that information with their initial writing at the beginning of their organizer where they wrote what they knew about the topic.

Conclude with the exit slip.

A Modern Perspective

Begin the lesson with a short social media post or extended headline about a current news event. It should give enough information for students to be able to identify a news topic and connect it with any contextual knowledge that they have, but be short enough to stimulate questions.

Consider using current news stories that have an identifiable perspective. If a news report tells a story from one perspective, while leaving another perspective identified but unreported, it presents opportunities for questions from students.

When using current news, consider having students search for their own additional news stories. As students engage with additional news stories to answer questions, encourage small groups to search a specific news source for their related news stories. Then have groups come together to share multiple news stories they found from their one news source as the story was reported on over time.

Differentiation

If working historically, students may need a small amount of contextual knowledge about a news event before they read the first news story. A secondary source such as a brief passage or even a historically based picture book can provide the introductory context that students may need.

Some students may struggle to multitask through multiple readings of an article to answer and then ask questions. If this is the case, assign some students to read the article to answer questions and other students to read the article to ask questions. These individual students may be partnered to share each other's work.

For a different element of contextual questioning, drop students into the middle of a news interview for a historical or current topic. As students create questions, they must also determine the context of the interview. Encourage students to use headlines and banners for additional information about a news event.

Questions may not all be answered by other news reports. Identify unanswered questions in historical or current iterations of this lesson and go beyond the news to find answers. Encourage students to identify reliable sources to find credible information to answer questions. Reach out to individuals, either historical experts if working with historical news or directly to the source or the news reporters themselves if working with current news.

Assessment

Exit Slip	
How did reading a news report with the task of asking questions change how you read the news story?	<u>Reading news to ask questions:</u>
How did reading a news story to answer questions change how you read and understood the news story?	<u>Reading news to answer questions:</u>

REFERENCES

"The End of Ballooning In the Army." *The Grand Haven News*, 20 Apr. 1864, https://chroniclingamerica.loc.gov/lccn/sn85033622/1864-04-20/ed-1/seq-2

"Research Guides: Civil War Ballooning: Topics in Chronicling America: Search Strategies & Selected Articles." Search Strategies & Selected Articles—Civil War Ballooning: Topics in Chronicling America—Research Guides at Library of Congress, guides.loc.gov/chronicling-america-civil-war-ballooning/selected-articles

Organizer

News Topic:
1. News Source:
2. What do you know from the story and from previous knowledge?
3. What do you want to know:
4. Select a question to answer:

5. New News Source:	What have you learned that can help answer this question?
	What new question do you have?

6. Select a question to answer:

7. New News Source:	What have you learned that can help answer this question?
	What new question do you have?

Lesson 10: Word Choice in the News

Words matter in the news. They set the tone of a news story and give the consumer of news clues about how to react to the events being reported. In divisive news, we can find examples of the same news event being reported on in two very different ways. Some of that can be attributed to the accompanying commentary (see Lesson 3: Differentiating Between News and News Commentary), but part of that difference in tone can be attributed to word choice.

For novice news consumers, the important takeaway is not that word choice should be stripped out of news reports and made neutral. What is more important to understand is that choices are being made when news reports and news scripts are written. Some of those choices are deliberate. Others may be products of cultural and social norms in large or small scopes. An example where word choice is used to report in a positive light is a news report of the local team using positive language to describe the team's efforts for the season.

This lesson asks students to look at word choice for a series of stories about Halloween pranks taking place at the turn of the 20th century. In this look at cultural norms in different parts of the United States at the time, students look at the language chosen to describe those pranks and connect that to the tone of the article. Students then select a different tone to represent and rewrite the article, keeping all of the facts but making different word choices to give the same story a different feeling or tone.

Objectives

In this lesson, students will:

- Determine a tone given to a news article or connected with the focus of a news article.
- Identify word choices within that news article that help to establish its tone.
- Rewrite a news article making deliberate word choices to alter the tone.

A Historic Perspective

Introduce the Lesson

Begin the lesson by asking students what may make two news reports on the same event different. Take all suggestions in a brief discussion with students. Transition by sharing that today's lesson is going to focus on the specific words chosen within a news story. Select a news story on Halloween pranks from the turn of the 20th century. Several have been suggested in the reference list within this lesson.

Begin the Activity

Ask students to read the news story and identify a tone or attitude that is conveyed through the reporting. Students can share their identified tones with the class without explanation. Students may change their selection of tones and document their selected tones in the organizer.

Next, ask students to perform a class reading on the news story using a lens of word choice. Specifically, ask students to identify words or short phrases that help to set the tone within the news story. Remind students that they may also look at the headline through the lens of word choice. Students can document their choices in the organizer or annotate directly on the news article.

Break the class into small groups where students have identified the same or similar tone to the article. Ask them to take a short amount of time to share and discuss their findings from the close reading analysis of the article. Then have students from those same small groups break into groups of two.

Invite the pairs of students to select an alternative tone for the same story they just analyzed. Suggest that it should be noticeably different from the tone of the original news story but also appropriate for the facts of the article. Then ask students to brainstorm a list of alternative words and phrases that could help support their chosen tone. Students may find it helpful to refer to their original list for inspiration.

After pairs of students have brainstormed a list of words, ask them to revisit the original article. Challenge them to rewrite the article to match their newly chosen tone. Students may use the words they just brainstormed together or may use different words and phrases. Remind students that the facts of their news story must stay the same. No additional "facts" may be added to the story that are not in the original article. Also, tell students that they may select phrases or even sentences from the original article to use directly in their own.

Discussion and Ending the Activity

After pairs of students have written their story, ask them to return to their earlier small groups to share their re-envisioned news story with others in the group.

End the lesson with the exit slip.

A Modern Perspective

In addition to word choice, how those words are said can make a difference. Consider using a broadcast news clip to identify word choice as well as delivery. Students can script and record an alternative broadcast to show a tone different from the original.

If working with a local news choice, consider reaching out to the news station to ask a journalist tasked with writing the news scripts for the station to share insights about the process and take questions about word choice within the writing.

Differentiation

If time allows, ask students to read others' rewritten news stories. As they focus on word choice within these new stories, encourage them to share how they would label the tone in the rewritten story. Then reveal the intended tone from the student writer.

If students are more familiar with news reporting structure, have them construct a news story from scratch about a historical event. Students may support each other in this effort by collaboratively using primary and secondary sources to collect facts that could be used in the news report.

A specific tone can appeal to specific groups. Challenge students to identify a news event and corresponding groups of individuals that would be interested in or affected by the story. Students then write news stories for the same event with the same facts that appeal to those different groups. Warn students against the use of too much commentary and ask them to focus on word choice to set the tone.

Assessment

Exit Slip	
How does word choice affect a news story? What does word choice not change within a news story?	

REFERENCES

"Hallowe'en Pranks." *Clark Courier*, 4 Nov. 1903, https://chroniclingamerica.loc
.gov/lccn/sn85025371/1903-11-04/ed-1/seq-1

"Hallowe'en Pranks." *Maryland Independent*, 2 Nov. 1906, https://chronicling
america.loc.gov/lccn/sn85025407/1906-11-02/ed-1/seq-3

"Halloween Observed. Boys Play Pranks in Different Parts of City—School Party."
The Yakima Herald, 5 Nov. 1901, https://chroniclingamerica.loc.gov/lccn
/sn88085523/1901-11-05/ed-1/seq-3

"Mischievous Boys Held. Woman's Leg Broken, Gravestones Desecrated, School
Property Destroyed." *The Citizen*, 17 Nov. 1909, https://chroniclingamerica
.loc.gov/lccn/sn87078082/1909-11-17/ed-1/seq-3

Organizer

Source:
Describe the tone of this news story using a short word or phrase:
What specific words or short phrases used help to identify its tone?
Select an alternative tone for this news story:
Brainstorm alternative words or short phrases that may display this tone:
Rewrite the news article using different word choices to change the tone. Remember to keep all of the facts the same. You may choose to keep portions of the article identical to the original.

Lesson 11: Voices in the News: Finding Who Is Heard and Who Is Not

"History is written by victors." A quote attributed to Winston Churchill may also be said about the news. Watching, listening to, and reading news from many sources will reveal that news has a voice. This can be seen in a variety of ways. News consumers can look at what news topics are being reported. They can observe the commentary that accompanies the story or the word choice within the story. The news has a voice, but it also tells the stories of individuals and groups. In that sense, those individuals' or groups' voices are prioritized. Other voices are left out or marginalized.

Voices should be taken into account by students developing news literacy. Identifying the voices that are represented in a news story helps students to see perspectives related to a news story. It also gives students an opportunity to look at voices that are connected with a news report but are not represented within that report. As part of identifying voices that are not represented, students can ask questions of these individuals or groups, giving students a reason to seek out more information on the news topic.

This lesson focuses on identifying voices within a news article about unemployment in urban and rural areas in the United States in October 1931. Students use a lens of close reading that focuses their attention on individuals and groups to identify voices related to the news story. Students expand that experience to ask questions about a voice that is mentioned in the news story but is not represented.

Objectives

In this lesson, students will:

- Analyze a news article through a close reading analysis to identify individuals and groups connected to the story.
- Identify a central voice represented in a news story and support their decisions with evidence.
- Identify a voice connected to a news story but not represented and support their decisions with evidence.
- Ask questions of an unrepresented or underrepresented voice in a news story related to information from the article.

A Historic Perspective

Introduce the Lesson

Begin the lesson by asking students about a memorable moment in the news, either current or historical. As students share, point out the individual or group that is the central focus of the news story. Transition by sharing that while there is a focus, there is also at least one other person or group connected to each story that we may not hear about.

Tell students that they are going to explore the voices that are represented in a news story connected with the Great Depression. Ask students what they know about that time in American history to create a collective context for students to draw from when they read the upcoming article.

Begin the Activity

Distribute the article "Warns Jobseekers Against Migration: Secretary Doak Says Urban Centers Only Able to Care for Own Unemployed" from the October 9, 1931 *Evening Star* along with the organizer. Ask students to analyze the article using a close reading strategy through a lens of individuals and groups connected to the story. Ask students to make direct quotes in the organizer or annotate in the article.

Using their findings from the close reading, students should next determine what individual or voice is most represented in the news story. If students struggle with this question, ask them to consider which individual or group represented in the article would agree with it the most. Ask them to use the organizer also to share evidence. Check in as a class to see what students determined to be the predominant voice in the story. It is likely that most, if not all, will have chosen Secretary of Labor Doak. If another individual or group was selected, ask students to support their idea with evidence from the article.

Next, ask students to identify an individual or group that was identified in the story but that the students felt had a voice that was not represented or underrepresented in the article. Again, ask students to support their decision with evidence from within the article. Remind students that evidence may include another individual speaking for them or about them when they do not speak. Again, ask students to share their ideas. There may be multiple choices here, including the unemployed, rural unemployed, urban unemployed, employers, or others. Ask students to support their choices with evidence from the news article.

For the final part of the analysis, ask students, in pairs, to identify questions that they would like to ask someone from the unrepresented or underrepresented group.

Discussion and Ending the Activity

With remaining time, ask students to share those questions with another pair or with the class.

End the lesson with the exit slip.

A Modern Perspective

Directly interacting with voices that are not included in a story can be a powerful lesson in appreciating and understanding all facets of a news topic beyond what the news report shares. For upper elementary and middle school students, target this lesson with an article or report from the high school newspaper or broadcasting club. They can identify a voice associated with the story that is underrepresented and develop questions. Those students can reach out to that individual or group to gather additional information related to the original story.

Differentiation

Students can also contextualize the news topic by reflecting individually and then sharing in small groups or as a class. The objective of contextualizing is for students to draw out what they know or believe they know about a topic. When they interact with news reports, they are then more likely to make connections with and draw understandings from the news.

When working with historical or current news, one article that underrepresents a particular voice may lead to a search for other news reports that focus on that voice. Students' learning can be extended to include searching for other related articles that represent other voices. When those news reports cannot be found, students can research the individual or group to predict how the questions they generated may have been answered.

Assessment

Exit Slip	
Why would someone look for voices that are unrepresented or underrepresented in a news report?	

REFERENCE

"Warns Jobseekers Against Migration: Secretary Doak Says Urban Centers Only Able to Care for Own Unemployed." *Evening Star*, 9 Oct. 1931, https://chroniclingamerica.loc.gov/lccn/sn83045462/1931-10-09/ed-1/seq-10/.

Organizer

Source:	
Close Reading:	
Whose voice is represented in this news report?	Direct quotes to support decision:
Whose voice is not represented in this news report?	Direct quotes to support the need to include this voice:
What questions could be answered by the missing voice in this news report?	

INTERACTING WITH THE NEWS

We do not only analyze news. We also interact with it. These lessons give novice news consumers opportunities to explore and discuss how to interact with news stories to make the experience meaningful and productive. These lessons focus on both interacting with the news and reaching beyond the news to learn more about the same topic. This includes reading multiple news stories on the same topic, reading stories over time to see the progression of a news topic, and going outside of the news altogether to more direct sources of information.

Lesson 12: Reading Across Headlines
Lesson 13: Curating Sources: Expanding Beyond an Initial View
Lesson 14: Going to the Source: Finding Primary Sources
Lesson 15: Making Connections Between News Topics: Cause and Effect
      in the News
Lesson 16: Stick with the Story: Following News over Time
Lesson 17: The Quick Share: Sharing, Liking, and Commenting on News

Lesson 12: Reading Across Headlines

Headlines are important in how people interact with news today. How many people do we know who react to a news story someone else has shared on social media just because they read the headline but not the entire news story? These headlines aren't just in print. Watching news stories that autoplay while viewers scroll past them, or having the television on with no sound, are additional opportunities for young consumers of news to see headlines.

This lesson encourages students to take the first step of corroborating a news story by looking beyond the one headline to view other headlines on the same news topic, specifically the sinking of the *USS Algonquin* in August of 1917. More than just viewing, though, they are tasked with thinking through the messages in the headlines to come to an initial understanding of the event being reported. Ultimately, students should realize that there is more beyond the headline, not only in the story itself but also in the wider news being reported.

Objectives

In this lesson, students will:

- Identify key words and phrases in a news headline.
- Look for patterns across multiple headlines on a topic.
- Create a general understanding of a news event based on a close reading of headlines.
- Ask questions generated by their close reading experience that they want to be answered by reading the news story.

A Historic Perspective

Introduce the Lesson

Collect at least a dozen headlines from a single news story associated with an event related to the students' content curriculum. For this lesson, students will use headlines from the sinking of the *USS Algonquin*, but headlines from any event could be used.

Gather at least 15 headlines concerning an event from various newspapers. These should be isolated from the news story. To give an authentic feel to the headlines, take screenshots of the headlines and print them out. Headlines can also be typed and printed in large strips.

Tell students that headlines can give readers a partial understanding of a news story, but will not give us all of the information we may want or need to understand the story. Ask students how they might find out more, other than reading the story associated with the headline. If no one shares the possibility of reading other news stories, suggest that option.

Begin the Activity

Tell students they are going to be reading through multiple headlines about the same news story. They are going to use a close reading technique to come to an initial understanding of the story.

Give each student two to three headlines from the event. There should be at least 15 headlines in total to assure a wide variety of content across the class. Students may work alongside each other with the same headlines, but should document their own initial findings. Headlines may vary greatly in length. Consider varying student headlines based on their individual needs at the moment of the lesson.

Ask students to read their headlines and mark individual words or short phrases (typically two to three words), that they react to strongly. Remind students that the headlines are short, so there may be a tendency to want to highlight the entire headline. Encourage them to be critical viewers as they read. Students should only need two to three minutes to mark their headlines.

After students have reacted to their individual headlines, ask them to share words or short phrases with the class. Document those in a place where the entire class can see them. Accept all student responses.

Ask students how they might organize this cluster of words and phrases. Have students, working in small groups of three to four, take the words and short phrases that were shared and group them. Tell students:

- Not all words and phrases have to be used.
- Words and phrases may be used in multiple groups.
- Groups of words and phrases can be of varying sizes.

As students begin grouping the words and phrases, ask them to title each of the groups to help others understand why each specific group was put together. As students finish their grouping of words and phrases, give an opportunity for several to share out the labels they gave their groups. Ask others if they created similar groups. In our example, students may create a group of words that elicit emotion, a group that refers to a ship, or a group that refers to Germans.

Then give students the most basic sentence possible about the event reported. For this example, it could be, "A ship sank." Ask students to replace or add a word or short phrase from the starter sentence with a word or short phrase from the initial large group of marked headline words and phrases. Tell students that the goal is to share what they know about the event just from reading headlines. For example, a student may replace the word *ship* with the word *steamer* so that the sentence reads, "A steamer sank." Another student may add the word *American* so that the sentence reads, "An American steamer sank." Continue replacing and expanding words until students are satisfied with the final statement.

Discussion and Ending the Activity

After students create their statement from the headlines, ask students what else they would like to know about the story. Document their responses. Ask where they might find out more after reading headlines. As a student suggests reading the news story itself, ask whether they should expect to find out everything from one news story.

Complete the lesson with the exit slip.

A Modern Perspective

Complete the same activity with a modern news story. Headlines grouped around a single topic can be found by searching a news topic at news.google .com or other aggregated news sites. Headlines can also be found in runners at the bottom of video stories. If tying into social media, students may also interact with the one or two sentences sometimes shared in a social networking post or Tweet about a news story.

If students already have an awareness of the event, encourage them to use their previous understanding to help create their groupings of words and shape the expanded sentence. They should not use their own language in any part of the activity where words from the headlines are to be used.

Differentiation

Using a slightly different analysis strategy, students could build knowledge across headlines more slowly, first comparing the analysis results of two headlines, reflecting on what they have corroborated and asking questions about what they have not. Then, students can add another headline and repeat the same process. This will take more time, but may more accurately reflect the real-world process novice news consumers may use outside of the school setting.

If content is more flexible, students may start with a very broad subject or topic. Ask them to document what they know about the topic. Differentiate student experiences by taking one area mentioned and finding a group of related headlines. This may be an option to introduce an individualized research project.

Assessment

Exit Slip	
How does a headline help us understand a news story? How can only reading a headline or headlines stop us from fully understanding a news story?	

REFERENCES

The Bridgeport Evening Farmer. 14 Mar. 1917, https://chroniclingamerica.loc.gov/lccn/sn84022472/1917-03-14/ed-1/seq-1

The Butte Daily Post. 14 Mar. 1917, https://chroniclingamerica.loc.gov/lccn/sn85053058/1917-03-14/ed-1/seq-1

Evening Star. 14 Mar. 1917, https://chroniclingamerica.loc.gov/lccn/sn83045462/1917-03-14/ed-1/seq-1

The Evening World. 14 Mar. 1917, https://chroniclingamerica.loc.gov/lccn/sn83030193/1917-03-14/ed-1/seq-1

Harrisburg Telegraph. (n.d.). https://chroniclingamerica.loc.gov/lccn/sn85038411/1917-03-14/ed-1/seq-1

The Ogden Standard. 14 Mar. 1917, https://chroniclingamerica.loc.gov/lccn/sn85058396/1917-03-14/ed-1/seq-1

The Richmond Palladium and Sun-Telegram. 14 Mar. 1917, https://chroniclingamerica.loc.gov/lccn/sn86058226/1917-03-14/ed-1/seq-1

Rogue River Courier. 14 Mar. 1917, https://chroniclingamerica.loc.gov/lccn/sn96088180/1917-03-14/ed-1/seq-1

Organizer

Take the shared words and short phrases from the news headlines and put them into groups. Words and phrases can be used more than once or not used at all. Give each group a name to show why the words and phrases are grouped together.

Group:	Group:
Group:	**Group:**
Group:	**Group:**

Lesson 13: Curating Sources: Expanding Beyond an Initial View

Expanding their understanding of a news story by looking beyond the first story they interact with is the one thing that students should learn to do consistently. It is touted by Sam Wineburg as an important skill for information-literate individuals (Wineburg, 2018). Of course, there are nuances to this task that involve close analysis of news, questioning, and considering elements of reliability and credibility. The truth is that if those considerations do not result in students widening their scope when considering a news story, they have missed a critical element.

While this book does not tackle fake news or conspiracy news directly, if educators wanted to explore that topic with their students, this would be an anchor lesson to use in those efforts. False reporting and unreliable sources are revealed more quickly when topics are deliberately searched more broadly.

In this lesson, students are given an initial news story. It is intentionally vague, but also intentionally encourages them to draw conclusions about the individuals and actions being reported. In this case, the resources are news reports about John Brown's 1859 raid on Harper's Ferry. Students are first asked to share reactions to the news. Then they are invited to learn more by curating their own information across multiple news sources. Students then reflect on the benefit of reading beyond the first story.

Objectives

In this lesson, students will:

- React to an initial news story.
- Identify additional news stories on a single topic to expand their understanding.
- Gather additional information and confirm or refute prior information by reading multiple news stories.
- Come to a consensus on events and individuals surrounding a news story.

A Historic Perspective

Introduce the Lesson

Give students a scenario: It is October 21, 1859. They pick up a newspaper from earlier in the week. A short article catches their attention. After reading the news article, their curiosity is piqued. They have an emotional reaction to the article. Ask students: If this same scenario happened with a piece of news today, what would they do? Invite a short discussion. If the possibility is not offered by students, suggest that some people might seek out more news on the topic.

Begin the Activity

Distribute the short article on Harper's Ferry from the October 18, 1859, issue of the *Penny Press*. Ask students to analyze the article individually using the provided organizer. They will be reading through multiple lenses, looking for facts but also looking at themselves as news readers to see how they feel about the events of the story and what questions they have. Guiding questions for their analysis could include:

- What is the news event being reported in this article?
- What are the important facts?
- How do they feel about the event? What text in the story led them to this?
- What questions do they have?

After they have done their analysis, invite students to share an element of fact, feeling, or question with the class. Collect these analysis points where all students can see them.

Ask students: What are the advantages or disadvantages of not reading more about a news topic? Students may share that not reading more about the topic will leave questions unanswered, that there may be more facts to know, or that feelings about the event and those involved may be changed or solidified if they sought out more news on this topic.

Show students the collection of articles from Chronicling America on Harper's Ferry. Remind them of the date in our scenario, October 21, 1859, and invite them, working with a partner or in small groups, to select an article from that date or earlier. If necessary, assign articles or portions of articles to pairs or small groups of students.

Invite students to read these articles with two goals. The first is to confirm or alter their feelings about the event. The second is to answer questions they had after the first article.

Share with students that each of the findings from the first news article may have new, confirmed, or dismissed pieces added to it. For example, a student could have an emotional reaction that made them sad that a group was causing trouble. After reading another article, the student could have a new feeling word or new evidence to explain the feeling of "sad." A student may also have confirmed their original feeling with new information. Lastly, a student could dismiss their original feeling because new information caused the original feeling of sadness to be replaced with a different feeling. These same options can happen with facts about the event and questions.

As students analyze new articles with a partner or in groups, continue to encourage them to document changes in their understanding of, feelings about, or questions regarding the news story using the organizer.

Ask students to explore a third article. If time does not allow, ask groups to report to each other to share new information from their article so that students have a third reporting of the event at Harper's Ferry. If time allows, ask for an example of new, confirmed, and dismissed information from each of the categories.

If previously working in pairs, consider now making groups of four. If working in small groups, keep those groups. Students, in their groups, should make a summary of their understanding of the events at Harper's Ferry from October 1859.

Discussion and Ending the Activity

Ask students how their understanding of the event changed after reading an additional article and gathering information from others' articles.

End the lesson with the exit slip.

A Modern Perspective

With current news stories, students may use news aggregators, such as Google News, to find multiple stories on the same event, topic, or individual.

Because news can unfold over time for more complex news events, this lesson may take several days. The students or the teacher may also collect news stories over several days and look back on the collection as a whole to analyze. As these more complex stories unfold, encourage students to be creative in their search for news stories. Identifying keywords for searches—a key skill in information literacy in general—can play an important role here.

Be sure to consider a variety of formats for current news. Online written stories, video reports, segments from broadcast news, and even social media reports from reliable sources can be brought together for a more complete understanding of a story.

Differentiation

Depending on time and student stamina with longer articles, students may be given parts of articles to jigsaw their understanding of a single news report. Educators can use their knowledge of their students to set this element up prior to the lesson if desired.

If students are practiced at searching a news database, encourage them to search for their own articles, individually, in pairs, or in small groups. More time will have to be allowed, but identifying their own news sources will broaden their understanding of the event.

Give students groups of news articles or ask students to search for news articles from different regions or different states. Ask:

- Do regions or states cover this news story differently?
- Are different facts or perspectives shared?
- Do certain newspapers provide greater coverage of this event than others? Is there any evidence of why this may be?

Assessment

Exit Slip	
If you read one news story and never read anything else on that news event, what could the consequences be?	

REFERENCES

"Insurrection Among the Slaves." *The Penny Press*, 18 Oct. 1859, https://chroniclingamerica.loc.gov/lccn/sn85025750/1859-10-18/ed-1/seq-1

"Research Guides: Harper's Ferry: Topics in Chronicling America: Search Strategies & Selected Articles." Search Strategies & Selected Articles—Harper's Ferry: Topics in Chronicling America—Research Guides at Library of Congress, Library of Congress, guides.loc.gov/chronicling-america-harpers-ferry/selected-articles

Organizer

<table>
<tr><td colspan="3">News Event:</td></tr>
<tr><td colspan="3">News Source:</td></tr>
<tr><td>Important Facts</td><td>Important Feelings</td><td>Important Questions</td></tr>
<tr><td></td><td></td><td></td></tr>
<tr><td colspan="3">Direct quotes in the news source connected to those facts, feelings, and questions.</td></tr>
<tr><td></td><td></td><td></td></tr>
<tr><td colspan="3">Additional News Source:</td></tr>
<tr><td>Changes in Facts (new, confirmed, or dismissed)</td><td>Changes in Feelings (new, confirmed, or dismissed)</td><td>Changes in Questions (new, confirmed, or dismissed)</td></tr>
<tr><td></td><td></td><td></td></tr>
<tr><td colspan="3">Direct quotes from the additional news source connected to changes in facts, feelings, and questions.</td></tr>
<tr><td></td><td></td><td></td></tr>
</table>

Lesson 14: Going to the Source: Finding Primary Sources

A *primary source* is any item directly related to a topic of study and the related time period. Technically speaking, then, news reports are primary sources. I certainly use them as primary sources with my students. But the point of this lesson is to look for other types of primary sources related to the same topic as the news we are using. Categorizing by formats, this could include interviews, photographs, raw video footage, and/or other types of items. The information from these types of items make up news reports and directly affect what news consumers think about a news event. It would not be unusual to see these types of primary sources mentioned within news reports.

One might ask, if a primary source is directly related to a topic of study, then aren't newspapers secondary if they are someone's interpretation of the event? No. All primary sources are, in some way, a person's interpretation of a moment, event, or time period. A person being interviewed is giving their account, but it is personal to them and influenced by how they viewed that moment. Even a photograph is influenced by a person's perspective. Individuals make a decision about where they point the camera, the focus of the photo, and what is left completely left out of the photo. None of these sources should be discounted because they are someone's interpretation. It is up to us to use those accounts to build our own understanding of the moment. The same is true with the news as a primary source.

The advantage of looking beyond other news reports when delving deeper into a news story is that it gives another opportunity to corroborate the story itself and often expands students' understandings of the story beyond what a short news report may provide. In this lesson, students look at a reported letter from a WWI soldier and then corroborate and expand their understanding of that event with the same soldier's diary.

Objectives

In this lesson, students will:

- Predict other formats of primary sources that could further inform them about a news report.
- Perform a close reading of a news story and diary.
- Corroborate information across two sources.
- Report on their expanded understanding of corroborating accuracy of a news report through the analysis of a primary source.

A Historic Perspective

Introduce the Lesson

Remind students that one important part of interacting with the news is corroborating news stories across multiple news reports. Ask students what else, besides news reports, could help them understand more about a news event.

Share that there are other sources that can help them understand the elements of news stories, called primary sources. If they are unfamiliar with primary sources, tell students that these items are directly related, in this case, to the news story itself. For example, if there was a news story on a fire at a local business, an interview with the business owner or firefighters would be considered a primary source. The building itself would be another primary source.

Begin the Activity

Provide each student with a copy of the organizer and a copy of the newspaper article, "Baltimore Troops Go 'Over The Top.'"

Invite students to read the news story provided. Ask small groups or partners to check in with each other on the topic of the story. As a whole class, remind students that the topic may vary depending on how we interact with the news story. Ask them to share possible topics. Expect students to share some of the following as topics: a WWI soldier; a shoot-out that an American soldier was in; WWI; a soldier from Baltimore; or the hardships of war.

Ask students what primary sources may be available that would help us understand this topic better. Give pairs of students an opportunity to select a topic and brainstorm a list of related primary sources. Quickly share out ideas.

Give students one topic, a soldier's life during WWI, as a possible topic. Ask students to read the article again, this time through the lens of identifying what information can be gained about that topic. Students can use the organizer to quote short phrases from the article and to summarize ideas.

Then give students a diary entry from the same soldier written about in the article. Ask students to read this diary entry for September 26, 1918. As with the news article, ask them to do a close reading through the lens of the life of a WWI soldier. Again, ask them to document their findings on the organizer.

Then ask students to compare the two close readings. Ask students to corroborate the articles to identify:

- Information that is the same in both sources.
- Information that is different or conflicting between the two sources.
- Information that only appears in one source.
- Questions they have about this soldier after reading both sources.

Discussion and Ending the Activity

Encourage students to share their findings in a whole-class discussion. Expand the discussion to include students' reflections on the two sources. Ask:

- What might more of this diary reveal about the topic being reported?
- How may primary sources be connected to news stories?
- How is your understanding of the accuracy of a news report affected by the analysis of primary sources?

End the lesson with the exit slip.

A Modern Perspective

Modern news reporting often has additional links or videos that may be considered primary sources of the news story. This can make a simple connection for corroborating the information in the story and encourage students to fully read, watch, and listen to information related to the news.

If working with local news, reach out to the news station to see if they have additional video or audio footage of an event or an interview. This primary source material can expand the students' understanding of the story as they analyze it.

If analyzing primary source video or news video, encourage students to include descriptions of what they see in addition to the words spoken. Emotional inflections, especially during interviews, can be helpful to document during the analysis process to fully investigate the source.

Differentiation

Think broadly about the types of sources that are directly connected to the news event and the time period. Numerical data as a primary source may directly affect how a student interprets a news story.

Consider including multiple primary sources with different perspectives into the analysis. This can encourage students to focus on facts or identify perspectives within the news story.

If students are more advanced in their searching of resources, encourage students to identify their own primary sources connected to a news event. This may also be accomplished with longer or multiple lessons and additional support from the teacher.

Assessment

Exit Slip	
How is corroborating a news story with primary sources different from corroborating with additional news reports? What do you think would be an ideal way to check the accuracy of a news story through corroboration?	

REFERENCES

"Baltimore Troops Go 'Over The Top.'" *Baltimore News*, Oct. 1918, http://memory.loc.gov/diglib/vhp/story/loc.natlib.afc2001001.23600/pageturner?ID=pm0001001. *Place the name of the newspaper and the month and year "October, 1918" in the header or footer of the document.*

Frieman, Harry. "Diary of Harry Frieman." *Diary of Harry Frieman*, Veterans History Project, http://memory.loc.gov/diglib/vhp/story/loc.natlib.afc2001001.23600/pageturner?ID=pm0003001&page=21. *Pages 21–23; Place the text "Harry Frieman Diary" as well as the date "September 26, 1918" in the header or footer of the document.*

Organizer

News Topic and Date:

Contextualize: What do you know about this topic?

News Source:

Close Reading for Information from the News Source:

Additional Primary Source:

Close Reading for Information from the Primary Source:

Highlight in one color information that is found in more than one source. Use a second color to highlight information that is found in only one source.

Lesson 15: Making Connections Between News Topics: Cause and Effect in the News

News does not live in a bubble. News reports on a topic are constantly being formed as news changes. News topics do not live in a bubble, either. They are often interconnected with each other. Local events affect national trends and vice versa. Economic issues trend across time and geography. Even in entertainment news, the reports of movie production troubles can affect later stories about the number of people who want to see the movie.

News consumers may not always be able to draw a line directly connecting two news topics, but the more aware our students are about a variety of news events, the more likely it is that they will be able to connect one news topic to another.

The idea behind this lesson is akin to building students' background knowledge. The case to be made is that one way to build that background knowledge is for students to be interacting regularly with varied and appropriate news. In this lesson, students begin with a news story that contains a map of population growth and decline during the 1930s. A noticeable pattern of population decline in the Midwest can encourage questions about what caused the decline. Additional articles from the same decade are utilized to make connections between the population decline and the Dust Bowls of that decade.

Objectives

In this lesson, students will:

- Use geographic and text literacy to understand a news source.
- Ask questions after interacting with a news article.
- Connect information between news articles on different topics to answer questions.

A Historic Perspective

Introduce the Lesson

Ask students if they have ever been influenced by someone or something. Certainly they have. If students struggle with examples, share that something as simple as the weather outside influences your decision about what to wear that day. Next, ask if they have ever influenced someone or something. Again, take a few comments. Share with students that a news event, even one that happened years earlier, can influence later news events.

Begin the Activity

Begin the activity with a map from the September 22, 1940, *Evening Star* ("Population Gains"). Share with students that sometimes the news is shared through illustrations. Ask students, in pairs, to use map-reading skills with question prompts from the organizer. Students will make observations and ask questions raised by those observations.

As students finish investigating the map, ask them to share their understanding of the map and how they labeled the map with a news topic. Student offerings for the topic will likely have something to do with population growth or change. Come to a class consensus on the topic.

Next, return to the organizer and the questions students asked related to the map. Separate these questions into two categories: questions that would require research with sources prior to the article being written and questions that would require research with sources after the article was written. Share with students that for this lesson they will be focusing on a question that requires them to look at sources created prior to this 1940s news article. Tell students they are going to look for information about why a grouping of states (Oklahoma, Kansas, Nebraska, South Dakota, and North Dakota) declined in population during the 1930s. If this question was not put forward by a student, offer it as a focus for the next stage of the lesson.

Share a passage from the first page of the same newspaper in an article titled "U.S. Population 131,409,881, 7 Percent Gain" (McKee). Share the passage that identifies five of the six states that lost population due to the effects of the Dust Bowl.

Offer students two articles, "The Fight on the Dust Demon" from 1936 and "Dust Bowl Faces Dark Outlook" from 1939. Ask students to give each article a close reading through the lens of making connections with the 1940 article. Give each set of partners an opportunity to read each article. In addition to the close reading, ask each pair to label each article with a topic. Most will likely label the topic as the Dust Bowl or something closely related. Students' close reading annotations and topics can be recorded on the organizer.

Discussion and Ending the Activity

End the lesson with a discussion of how these two separate topics—population change in the 1930s and the Dust Bowl—are connected. Ask students to use evidence from the second two articles to support their ideas.

Ask students to complete the exit slip.

A Modern Perspective

News stories around geography and weather patterns lend themselves to connecting multiple news topics. News stories about drought may, months later, be related to news stories about wildfires or failing crops. Economic news reports about insurance or grocery prices may connect with those earlier stories.

Consider taking a long-term approach to this lesson if making connections between different news topics over time. Students can regularly be browsing news aggregators for connecting news stories. When the reports themselves make the connections between different news topics, news aggregators can be searched using keywords from older news stories.

Differentiation

This lesson focuses on one specific question coming from a news story. Consider letting students search Chronicling America or other historical news databases to find news stories that can answer other student-developed questions.

Instead of presenting the news stories from the end of the timespan, present the news stories chronologically. Giving students a story from the beginning of the timespan, identify the news topic, and ask them to predict what effects could come from an identified cause in the news story.

Assessment

Exit Slip	
If the news is about current events, how does news from the past affect our understanding of news from today?	

REFERENCES

"Dust Bowl Faces Dark Outlook." *Evening Star*, 8 Dec. 1939, https://chronicling america.loc.gov/lccn/sn83045462/1939-12-08/ed-1/seq-55

"The Fight on the Dust Demon." *The Indianapolis Times*, 2 Apr. 1936, https:// chroniclingamerica.loc.gov/lccn/sn82015313/1936-04-02/ed-1/seq-17

McKee, Oliver. "U.S. Population 131,409,881, 7 Per Cent Gain." *Evening Star*, 22 Sept. 1940, https://chroniclingamerica.loc.gov/lccn/sn83045462/1940-09 -22/ed-1/seq-1

"Population Gains for Decade." *Evening Star*, 22 Sept. 1940, https://chronicling america.loc.gov/lccn/sn83045462/1940-09-22/ed-1/seq-5

Organizer

News Source:	
What do you notice about the source? Why was it created?	
What news is being shared?	
What is unusual or unexpected?	
What questions could you ask based on this source?	
What news topic would you use to label this source?	

Additional News Source 1:

What connections can you find with the first source?	
What news topic would you use to label this source?	

Additional News Source 2:

What connections can you find with the first source?	
What news topic would you use to label this source?	

Lesson 16: Stick with the Story: Following News over Time

News events change. How could they not? If we define news as *a broadcast or publication to inform about a recent event*, then we can expect more recent aspects of an event to add to our understanding developed from previous elements of the same event. Other lessons look at events over a time at the heart of the lesson or in differentiated suggestions.

There is another way in which news changes, though: through the revelation of new or more information about a single event. This appears to be more common in news reports surrounding chaotic or complex situations. In these instances, not all of the information can be gathered at once. There is a greater chance of a lack of information, misinformation, or mistake being communicated through a news report.

In our, and our students', reality of 24-hour news, this is even more likely to happen. News channels can be turned on at any moment. Headlines are pushed out to phones, watches, and other devices at all hours of the day. The term *breaking news* can lose its impact and blend into the background as information comes at us regularly.

As emerging news consumers, upper elementary and middle school students have a responsibility to revisit evolving news events that affect them or hold high interest for them. There are, of course, tragic unfolding events that we do not want our young students to be totally immersed in for their own social-emotional well-being. We do, however, want students to recognize that reporting the news can take time and that news consumers often actively seek out updates on news events or initial reporting.

In this lesson, students look back at an unfolding news event, the sinking of the *Titanic*. As you may imagine, the first reports were not as thorough as one might have hoped. Students will have the opportunity to see how reporting on an event that had already taken place evolved as new information was obtained and misinformation was corrected.

Objectives

In this lesson, students will:

- Identify the major information in multiple related news reports taking place over time.
- Corroborate information across multiple stories.
- Highlight conflicting information across news reports.
- Determine what information is most reliable based on the chronology of reporting and prior knowledge.

A Historic Perspective

Introduce the Lesson

Begin the lesson by asking students why they think reports on a news event might change over time, and why a news story on the same topic may be different later that day or the next day compared to an earlier report. Have a short discussion on student responses.

Tell students that they are going to investigate a news event over three days. Share that the news story was reported on for much longer than that, but their focus will be the first three days of the reporting. Their ultimate goal will be to return to the question that started the class.

Begin the Activity

Ask students if they know anything about the ship called the *Titanic*. Most likely many, if not all will know something. Ask students to take two to three minutes to share what they do know about this topic in the organizer. If necessary, encourage students to share their background information in a group of three.

In those same groups of three, students should access the front page of *The Detroit Times* for April 15th, 16th, and 17th of 1912. Each student, working independently, can do a close reading of one page of the newspaper. Ask students to scan the front page of their day of the newspaper and read any articles or other information related to the *Titanic*. Using the organizer, students can document information that they think is important or worth noting about the sinking of the ship.

After students have written down their close reading findings from their day of the newspaper, they can return to the group to share information from across the three days of reporting. Students should corroborate findings and focus on finding any conflicting information. They should also document conflicting information in the column to the right of their close readings findings, along with the corresponding date.

Students may return to the front page containing their articles if a teammate shares information but not all students wrote down related information. For example, if one student wrote the number of passengers lost at sea in the organizer but the other two did not, students should return to their newspapers to see if that was reported. If so, they should add it to their close reading findings and show how that information compares with the other two days of reporting.

Discussion and Ending the Activity

After students have corroborated their close readings, ask the class what major topics of conflicting information they found over the three days of reporting. Ask students to describe not only what information changed, but also how it changed over time. Finish the class discussion by asking students why they believe the information reported changed over the course of those three days. Ask all students to share their thoughts on their organizers.

Finish the lesson with the exit slip.

A Modern Perspective

This activity may be more safely done with recent news that has already been reported out over multiple days. Depending on the topic, reporting that is sensitive or disturbing to younger students may be released over time. Consider the topic being tracked before deciding to do this activity with real-time news reporting.

If tracking a local event, consider reaching out to a news reporter to inquire about how deadlines and schedules affect the accuracy of information being reported over time for a news story. Students may be interested to know how information is gathered over time by a news reporter for ongoing reporting purposes.

Some text-based news available online is updated over time to reflect changes in known information. Students may track news stories from a news site that gives these types of updates to understand another example of where evolving reporting of news is seen.

Differentiation

If at the point of this lesson students are more adept at independently analyzing newspaper articles, have groups of three each follow a different newspaper. This allows students to verify that one newspaper isn't missing available information, and to recognize that the information available to news agencies as a whole is similar.

If some elements of the news story are too sensitive for students or if a shorter lesson is needed, curate a single news article from the front page of the newspaper over three days. The articles over three days could be curated to focus on a single element of reporting on the broader news topic of the sinking of the *Titanic*. For example, a teacher could curate articles focused on the reported number of survivors to show the change in reporting over three days, without other details that may be too disturbing.

Assessment

Exit Slip
How would you react to a person sharing outdated information from a news event that you know has had new and updated information reported over time?	

REFERENCES

"The Detroit Times. (Detroit, Mich.) 1903–1920, April 15, 1912, AFTERNOON EDITION, Image 1." *News about Chronicling America RSS*, Detroit To-Day Co., chroniclingamerica.loc.gov/lccn/sn83016689/1912-04-15/ed-1/seq-1

"The Detroit Times. (Detroit, Mich.) 1903–1920, April 16, 1912, EXTRA, Image 1." *News about Chronicling America RSS*, Detroit To-Day Co., chronicling america.loc.gov/lccn/sn83016689/1912-04-16/ed-1/seq-1

"The Detroit Times. (Detroit, Mich.) 1903–1920, April 17, 1912, AFTERNOON EDITION, Image 1." *News about Chronicling America RSS*, Detroit To-Day Co., chroniclingamerica.loc.gov/lccn/sn83016689/1912-04-17/ed-1/seq-1

Organizer

<table>
<tr><td colspan="2">News Topic:</td></tr>
<tr><td colspan="2">Contextualize: What do you know about this topic?</td></tr>
<tr><td>First Source:</td><td>Date:</td></tr>
<tr><td>Close Reading First Source:</td><td>Conflicting Information from Other Sources (Include date of reporting):</td></tr>
<tr><td colspan="2">Why might information reported about the same news topic over three days be conflicting?</td></tr>
</table>

Lesson 17: The Quick Share: Sharing, Liking, and Commenting on News

One thing that has changed in the last 10 to 15 years with regard to the news is how it is shared. Now social media plays a large role in how people find their news. Whether through browsing or notifications, news reports and sometimes misinformation, disinformation, or advertisements that have the appearance of news are put in front of people. Some of that sharing comes from reliable sources. News outlets have their own presence on social media.

Much news found on social media is shared by news messengers though. We have become not just news consumers but news messengers as well. What becomes tricky is that our own reputations as friends, relatives, professionals, and colleagues to our connections on social media may play a role in how the news we share is perceived. Similarly to news sources establishing reliability or trustworthiness, people on social media who distribute news also have varying degrees of trustworthiness for their online followers and friends. Commentary added to the sharing of news on social media likely affects this trustworthiness.

Another element that can affect how news is shared on social media is the quick pace of browsing and sharing. News reports in all formats are shared and "liked" regularly. "Likes" often imply approval of the content of the news story, the individual or organization that created it, or the individual sharing it. In this lesson, students will share historical news topics in a simulated social media space.

Objectives

In this lesson, students will:

- Simulate sharing a news story and reacting to news reports on social media.
- Reflect on their role as news messengers on social media.
- Collectively suggest best practices for sharing and reacting to the news on social media.

A Historic Perspective

Introduce the Lesson

For this lesson, students will need access to several collections of news stories to quickly browse and select from. These can be curated prior to the lesson to be targeted on one topic. A selection of collections from the "Recommended Topics" page on Chronicling America could be used. Educators may want to select collections from the "Recommended Topics" page because not all listed topics are appropriate for upper elementary and middle school students.

Begin the lesson by gauging students' experience with social media. Ask any students if they are on social media. For those who are, ask if they ever see news on social media and if they ever interact with it. Let students' experiences lead this discussion to provide a shared understanding with the class.

If it does not come up through classroom conversation, tell them that some people sometimes share and like items on social media, including news, very quickly as they scroll through items shared. Ask students for examples of types of news they might find themselves sharing with friends on social media even if they are not currently on social media. Tell students that they will see what this can look like with sharing the news through social media.

Begin the Activity

This simulation can take place in a few ways. Items can be done completely with printed articles and printed charts with opportunities for students to respond. The lesson can also be done online if students can access articles through provided links and have access to an online classroom environment where they can make posts and comment on other's posts. Lastly, it could be a hybrid where some content is accessed or shared online and other parts are done in print. For our purposes, the lesson will follow an online model.

Give students a selection of collections of news stories with instructions to take five minutes to select a collection and then an article that they think is worth sharing with the larger community for any reason. After five minutes, give students 60 to 90 seconds to share the article using the selected class online platform. Encourage students to include some commentary that shares why they chose the article or why they believe other people should read it. As students are reading and posting news articles, the teacher should share photographs from earlier in the year or other appropriate photographs on the same platform.

As students finish posting their article, tell them that they will be browsing the online platform to see what others have shared. They are welcome to read, comment on, share, or like any posts. There is no set number of posts they have to interact with, but they should do this individually without talking with others. All communication should take place completely online. As students are reacting to the posts, the teacher should share additional photographs as well as a small number of news stories on the same online platform.

Discussion and Ending the Activity

After adequate time for students to interact with a number of the posts but not all, bring the class back together for a discussion. Tell the class that the goal of the discussion is to reflect on their interaction with news on the online platform to come up with recommended ways of interacting with the news. Begin by asking students:

- Why did you select the news report to share that you did?
- Approximately how many news stories did you interact with?

- How did the non-news sharing affect you as you were browsing online?
- How did you select which news reports you interacted with?
- How did you interact with the news reports? If students do not give the suggestion, ask them if they read the news reports that they commented on, liked, or shared.
- What caused you to comment on a news story versus liking or sharing it?

Point out practices that resulted in users not fully interacting with the news. Acknowledge that this happens in the real world as well. Ask students what suggestions they would give new users to social media when they are considering sharing a news story or see a news story that a friend shares.

End the lesson with the exit slip.

A Modern Perspective

When using current news for this simulation, students may each be given a news topic and search for a news story or use a category in a news aggregator to identify a news story to share.

Students may share current news stories, so other students may have some knowledge of the news topic being shared. That may result in more in-depth comments or even questioning of student commentary that accompanies the shared post.

Differentiation

If using an online experience for the online network, consider giving a few students a set of short video news reports as options. During the discussion, ask students if there was a format of news that was more appealing than another.

Consider the length of the written news story or video news story against the time allowed for the lesson. Students should have time to read or view news stories shared by others, although the amount of news they can fully interact with may vary greatly depending on the time available for the lesson.

Assessment

Exit Slip	
When seeing news shared by someone on posted media, what are ways to understand the news story that is shared?	

REFERENCE

"Topics by Subject." Topics Arranged by Subject from Topics in Chronicling America (Newspaper and Current Periodical Reading Room, Serial and Government Publications Division, Library of Congress), www.loc.gov/rr/news/topics /topicsSubject.html.

UNDERSTANDING ONESELF AND OTHERS AS NEWS CONSUMERS

We all bring our own perspective and experiences to engaging with the news. This final set of lessons gives students an opportunity to explore who they are as news consumers while also realizing that others may not react or interact with news in the same way. The final set of lessons gives students an opportunity to realize that they play an integral role as news consumers, that our opinions and reactions to the news have value, and that there is value to how others view the news as well.

Lesson 18: What Is My Opinion?: Being Aware of Our Own Biases
Lesson 19: Rethinking Relationships: Reflecting on Affinities with News Sources
Lesson 20: Interacting with and Reacting to Emotionally Charged News Topics
Lesson 21: How Will Others Read This?: Predicting Audience Viewpoints

Lesson 18: What Is My Opinion?: Being Aware of Our Own Biases

If we have some understanding of a news event, a person or group involved in that event, or even a related event, it is likely that we have some opinion or bias related to the news. It is not inherently wrong to have a bias. A student may have a bias toward underdogs who stick up for themselves. Another may have a bias toward educators because that is a parent's profession. Often we have a bias toward what we know and are comfortable with.

I want to address the word *bias*. For some, it has the meaning of being an unfair or unsubstantiated opinion. I do not use the term in this way with my students, but if you do, you may choose to substitute the word *perspective* for this lesson.

Biases and perspectives may not always be based on fact and they are often not directly related to a news story that we are consuming. These biases can influence how we perceive a news story. Our approval of one idea over another in a news report can be directly affected by our biases. Although it is difficult to stop that from happening, students can identify their own bias related to a news story. This is a step in identifying others' perspectives as an important element of news literacy.

In this lesson, students view a seven-minute news story about recycling. It is a topic that they will all know about and have some level of personal experience with. This, along with multiple perspectives within the story, will give the students an opportunity to identify their biases toward different elements and individuals within the story. It is important for students to already be familiar with the differences between facts and opinions before addressing biases.

Objectives

In this lesson, students will:

- Reflect on their personal feelings about the topic of a news story.
- Label individuals, messages, and ideas within a news story as positive or negative.
- Compare their labeling of parts of the news story to their feelings about the overall topic.

A Historic Perspective

Introduce the Lesson

Begin by asking students if they often have opinions about different aspects of their life. If unsure, share examples related to school, such as opinions about certain rules or traditions at the school. Acknowledge that when we have an understanding of or experience with something, we often form opinions about it. As an example, if we have a positive opinion about an actor and then hear a news report about a new movie that person will be in, it might be more likely that we will be excited about the movie. Our perspectives can influence how we feel about a news story.

If choosing to do so, introduce the word *bias*. *Bias* may be defined as a preference for an idea, person, or group. Biases cause us to judge something before we have fully understood or investigated it. Return to the movie example. I have not seen the movie but have a positive bias toward it because of one person in it.

Begin the Activity

Share with students that they will explore their own bias in how they react to a news story. Provide students with the organizer along with the topic of recycling. Ask them, on the organizer, to write a short description of their own positive or negative feelings on this topic.

Many students will likely write positive feelings about recycling and its importance. There may be opposing opinions, though. A student may have a negative feeling that more recycled material is not processed in the United States, for example. Another feeling may be that it takes too much time and effort. Be sure to acknowledge all opinions. Also ask students to rank the strength of their negative or positive feelings. Encourage them to think about others who may feel more or less strongly to gauge where they fall on a 1–5 scale.

After students have documented their opinion on the topic, introduce the news story on recycling from The MacNeil/Lehrer NewsHour on October 2, 1989. Instruct students that, as they watch the seven-minute report, they should identify spoken words or visual elements related to the topic that they are reacting to. As they do this, they should also identify whether their reaction is positive or negative and rank the strength of that reaction. If students struggle with what it means to react to an element of a news story, share that it is an element of the news story that they resonate with, connect to, or feel may be important in some personal way.

If possible, having students watch the provided clip individually or in pairs will allow them opportunities to rewatch segments of the story if necessary. Students may also watch as a whole class, but the segment may have to be shown twice. If students do not have navigational control of the news story, acknowledge that it may be difficult to react to and document everything they want to capture.

After students have had ample time to view the news story and document their reaction to it, ask students to share what they reacted to in small groups. Tell students to look for common elements they reacted to as well as elements of the news story that only one person documented a reaction to.

Discussion and Ending the Activity

Bring the class back to whole-group instruction. Ask students:

- Did everyone in your group react to the same elements of the news story? What were the common elements?

- Were there any elements that more than one person reacted to but one person reacted positively and another negatively? What might have caused these different reactions?
- Were there any elements where individuals both reacted positively or negatively but the scale was different? What might have caused these different reactions?

Close the lesson by asking students to compare the overall strength of their feelings about recycling to the individual ranks of their reactions. Ask students if they feel their reactions to individual segments were fairly similar to or fairly different from the strength of their feeling toward the topic overall. Allow students to comment.

End the lesson with the exit slip.

A Modern Perspective

Because students may be more closely involved with current news stories, they also may hold stronger biases and opinions on the topics. That can make it more difficult to identify their own biases. In selecting a current news story for this lesson, try to predict students' perspectives and select a topic that students may not be as strongly invested in. As students become more adept at identifying their own biases, news they are more invested in can be explored.

Most students have strong opinions about some current news topics. Ask students to identify a news topic about which they feel strongly. Then, using a news aggregator, have them individually react to the first news story from a search. Ask them to partner with another student with a less strong feeling about the topic. Pairs can swap news stories and compare the results of their reactions.

Differentiation

Some news stories may not show two or more perspectives within the story. If this is the case, consider pairing multiple news stories that show different perspectives. This will make it easier for students to react and compare with their overall bias for or against the topic.

Our biases toward a news story can be provoked by the headline, news story introduction, or even the graphic accompanying the story. Consider using one of those elements as the topic for students to react to when beginning the lesson.

In addition to the topic, how the topic is presented can affect how student biases come into play. As an extension activity, encourage students to rewrite news stories (on the same topic) with different language that they feel would cause an altered reaction. Students should be careful not to change the facts of the story, only how those facts are presented.

Assessment

Exit Slip	
How likely is it that others who see the same news reports as you have the same reaction to it? Why do you think this?	

REFERENCE

"The MacNeil/Lehrer NewsHour." NewsHour Productions, American Archive of Public Broadcasting (WGBH and the Library of Congress), Boston, MA and Washington, DC. 2 Oct. 1989. https://americanarchive.org/catalog/cpb-aacip -507-0g3gx4590c?start=2782.19&end=3240.72

Organizer

Topic:		
Your Feeling on This Topic:		
Using a 1–5 scale, how strongly do you feel about this topic?		
News Story Language or Visual	Positive or Negative	1–5 Scale

Lesson 19: Rethinking Relationships: Reflecting on Affinities with News Sources

Many of us have our preferred news sources. These news sources become preferred for a variety of reasons: sometimes because it is a local source, because it report on topics of interest, or because a favorite reporter or anchor works for the news source. Students too are likely to develop, or may have already developed, preferred news sources, although they may live on platforms that we adults may use less frequently for news, such as YouTube or a social media platform.

There is a benefit to branching out beyond a preferred few news sources, though. The most important is that it allows news consumers an opportunity to corroborate information and interact with news stories that come from different perspectives. Taking news from a larger number of news producers also helps news consumers make decisions about a news source's reliability or trustworthiness.

In this lesson, students reflect on favorite places to get their news on topics that are meaningful to them. They also simulate getting their news from just one source through an activity in which individual students search for a news story from a specific state on the topic of the Alaskan Gold Rush of the late 19th century. Students will compare results and do additional searches within their selected newspaper over time on the same topic to hypothesize what might happen if they only read news from that single news source.

Objectives

In this lesson, students will:

- Reflect on their own sources for news on topics that are of interest to them.
- Perform an advanced search of a historical news database.
- Compare elements found in a common news story from newspapers across the United States.
- Discuss the limitations of using only one news source.

A Historic Perspective

Introduce the Lesson

For this activity, students will need to have an individual device with internet access.

Begin by asking students if they have a favorite source of news for a particular topic that they follow. Students may share a news source for movies, video games, local events, or weather news. Invite a small number of students to share why they typically use the same news source for that topic.

Begin the Activity

Tell students that they will be taking a historical look at using a single news source around the topic of the Alaskan Gold Rush. Ask students to use their device to access Chronicling America. As a group, guide students through the process of accessing the Advanced Search tab from the main page. Also guide students to limit the search year to 1890 and the search terms "gold" and "Alaska" using the "within 5 words of each other" option.

Using the results, assign each student an article from a different newspaper. Students should use the organizer to record the topic and specific newspaper and date that they will be reading. Ask students to do a close reading of the article through a lens of understanding. Students may print out the article to annotate on it and use the organizer to summarize key ideas and understandings from the article.

After students have done a close reading of their article, ask them to imagine that this was the only news source they had on this topic. Now ask individuals within the group to share one key idea or understanding they took away from the article. When sharing, ask students to also share the newspaper, along with its city and state, as well as the date of the article. As students listen, ask them to select five pieces of information that were not in the article they read and document it along with the publication date of the newspaper article it came from.

Return to the Advanced Search page within Chronicling America. Guide students in doing another search. Ask students to repeat the search parameters from their first search. In addition, they should limit their search to the selected newspaper their article was printed in.

Invite students to identify how many days in that year the topic was reported on in their selected newspaper. Next, ask them to sort results by date and try to find newspaper reports in their newspaper from a similar time as a news story that someone shared earlier. Students may find very different articles. Others may find the exact same article as a classmate that is reprinted in multiple newspapers. In small groups, ask students to share some of their findings.

Discussion and Ending the Activity

After a brief small group discussion, bring students back to the whole class. Ask students:

- What does the varying number of stories tell you about how news is reported from different sources?
- When you read a story from your selected newspaper from a specific date or date range, did you find similar information compared to what a classmate found in that same date range in a different newspaper?
- What does this tell you about news sources?
- What should those of us who are news consumers consider when we think about what we found today?

End the lesson with the exit slip.

A Modern Perspective

Depending on the topic being searched in the news and the news sources, educators may find that students have preconceived notions about some media outlets. Some news stories can be sensitive for students. Select the topic for this activity with these issues in mind.

Seek out local news sources from across the country to search for news topics. Curate a group of websites or social media handles for students to search for a specific current news topic. A school's local news source, either print or television, may be willing to have a representative speak with students about how their company makes decisions about what news is reported and how it is presented to news consumers.

If following a news topic in real time, students can complete the second part of the historically based lesson over the course of days in short segments. Encourage students to document and link to sources as they share evolving news.

Differentiation

Students may have varying degrees of stamina and different reading abilities. Pre-assigning articles of varying lengths and vocabulary can give students a successful experience during the close reading and allow them to share found information with the rest of the class. Students may also be partnered for additional support.

Begin the first search by showing students how to limit a search by state. Give students different states in which to search for their search terms. They should continue to limit by date as well. This may be met with varying degrees of success depending on the topic that students are searching and how widespread the coverage of that topic was.

Depending on the topic, students may want to search by a date range shorter than one year. Depending on the urgency of the news, it was not unusual for news stories to spread more slowly across the United States in past centuries. An event may be reported up to two weeks later in the late 19th and early 20th century and still be considered new reporting of an event. Adjust date ranges for searches accordingly.

Assessment

Exit Slip	
What are the advantages or disadvantages of getting all of your news on a topic from one source?	

REFERENCE

National Endowment for the Humanities. "Chronicling America Advanced Search." *Chronicling America: Library of Congress*, chroniclingamerica.loc.gov/#tab =tab_advanced_search

Organizer

Topic:	
Source:	Date:

Close Reading of the Source:

Information from Other Sources	Source and Date

The number of articles on your topic for the year from original source:

Lesson 20: Interacting with and Reacting to Emotionally Charged News Topics

While the news, at its core, is meant to inform, some news topics can also affect us emotionally. Those emotions can vary widely. Stories of underdogs and triumphs can cause us to feel joy. News of injustices and loss can make us feel sadness or anger. Every other feeling can be brought forth from a news story as well.

There is some news that you may feel is inappropriate for your upper elementary or middle school students to interact with. There are times, though, when historical events are part of the curriculum or when sensitive topics in current events warrant discussion in the classroom. In both of these cases, news reports can be a way to inform students. This should be done while planning for possible emotional responses from students. Students becoming able to recognize and process their own feelings in a safe space at school is essential and necessary as students grow in their social-emotional health. In this instance, that growth may coincide with their growth in news literacy.

In this lesson, students investigate the role of news agencies related to the 1963 Birmingham Campaign, when more than a thousand students marched on the town to promote ideas around civil rights. Hundreds were arrested and force was used to stop the demonstrations. Photos and television news footage of fire hoses and police dogs brought forth an emotional response from many. Students experiencing this moment in history through the news reporting may experience similar emotions. Because it can be especially sensitive, the more graphic images and television footage of the time are not used in this lesson. The lesson gives one way to support students in their natural responses of feeling emotions while giving them an opportunity to process those emotions.

Objectives

In this lesson, students will:

- Prepare for an emotionally sensitive news report.
- Reflect on their own emotional reaction during and after the report.
- Identify the historical facts present in the news report.
- Make connections between historical facts and emotional responses.

A Historic Perspective

Introduce the Lesson

Begin by acknowledging to students that the day's lesson may be challenging because it asks students to talk about emotions, something that is not always easy to do. Also, share that they are being asked to talk about those emotions because they are connected to a very important historical news topic.

Students likely have some familiarity with the broader topic of the civil rights movement. Begin by sharing the picture book *Let the Children March* by Monica Clark-Robinson and Frank Morrison. This book or other sources can be used to give context to the news reports. Ask students to listen to the story through a lens of understanding the events. Students should use the Background Source portion of the organizer to quote short phrases from the book that illustrate the event. Ask students to share their understanding of the event according to the report to build a shared understanding among the class.

Begin the Activity

Next, tell students that they will be reading a news commentary that contains information from this same event. Tell students that they will be reading this news report through two lenses. One lens will be of importance, documenting the words that appear to be important to the story being reported. The other lens will be one of emotion, describing what emotions are being felt while reading the article. Tell students that some emotions may already be present after hearing the picture book. Those may change to a different emotion, continue to be the same emotion but elevate or decrease, or not change at all. Multiple emotions may also be felt at the same time.

Distribute the cover of the May 10, 1963 issue of the *Arizona Tribune*. After students read the news article, give them time to reflect on their emotions and document them in their organizer.

Ask students to make connections between the events in the news report and their emotions. Invite them to draw arrows between items they have listed in each row of the organizer. If they feel something is missing, encourage them to add it. Let them know that not everything has to be connected. Encourage them to identify the connections they see.

Now invite students to reflect on other elements of their life or prior knowledge that may affect those connections between the news story and emotions. For example, if students have felt mistreated and read the way these young protesters were treated, they may feel angry. Ask students to return to documenting in their organizer.

Move to the last resource, a short clip from *The American Revolution of '63* aired on NBC in September of 1963. Tell students that they will be watching this to look for any evidence of how others may have reacted emotionally to the events in Birmingham. Ask students to watch the short clip through a lens of identifying emotions. As students find words and phrases that convey emotions, they can document them in the organizer.

Discussion and Ending the Activity

Invite students to share their findings from the final resource with the class.

End the lesson with the exit slip.

A Modern Perspective

Discussing what students already know about a news story, as well as how they felt about the event reported, may be a more logical place to begin this lesson when working with current news. With students aware of the news of the day, students may already have had an emotional reaction to a news story prior to interacting with the news report in class. In some cases, especially if students read, listened to, or watched news stories independent of adults or peers, these students may not have processed their emotional reactions to the story.

Differentiation

The background source used at the beginning of the lesson can also be a news source that gives contextual information to students. If considering using news sources for both the initial piece and the main source of the lesson, consider which is better at conveying information and which is better at conveying emotion for students.

When utilizing this lesson with other topics, consider the impact of the news format being used. The combination of color footage and sound may be the most emotionally impactful for most students. Some students may benefit from watching the news footage with the sound off when there is no narration or interview. Black-and-white footage or lack of sound can provide more separation from the emotional impact. A text-only news report can provide the most separation.

Assessment

Exit Slip	
What do you think is a useful skill for you to use when interacting with a news story that may be difficult to watch, listen to, or read?	

REFERENCES

The American Revolution of '63. NBC, 2 Sept. 1963, https://loc.gov/exhibits/civil-rights-act/multimedia/television-and-birmingham.html

Clark-Robinson, Monica, and Frank Morrison. *Let the Children March.* HMH Books for Young Readers, 2018.

"The Shame of Birmingham." *Arizona Tribune*, 10 May 1963, https://chronicling america.loc.gov/lccn/sn84021918/1963-05-10/ed-1/seq-1

Organizer

Background Source:	
What did you read/see/hear that helps to explain the event?	

Main News Source:	
What did you read/see/hear that you felt was important to understanding the news report?	
What emotions did you experience when you were interacting with the news report?	
What personal experiences or other events may be affecting the emotions you felt?	
What questions do you now have about this event?	

Final Source:	
What evidence of others' emotions can be found in this source? Use words, short phrases, or descriptions to document what you find.	

Lesson 21: How Will Others Read This?: Predicting Audience Viewpoints

One area of news literacy that is often less developed with upper elementary and middle school students is recognizing the potential viewpoints of other news consumers. There is an amount of empathy that plays a role in being able to predict how others may feel about a subject in the news and why they may feel that way. It is an important skill to develop, though. Being able to recognize and begin to understand the perspective of another individual is essential for healthy discourse around the news of the day. I also believe that when we can recognize those differences in perspectives, we are drawn to find common ground. An alternative is to simply dismiss others as "wrong" because they disagree with you. Understanding is a better course.

This is not meant to imply that every perspective is of equal value. There are perspectives that are grounded in prejudice. Others may be based on misinformation. When it comes to the news of the day, when those viewpoints reveal themselves, recognizing where they come from can, at the very least, help to explain the origins of a perspective.

This lesson uses a news report on the gas shortages of 1979. It contains a number of brief statements by people affected by the shortages. This gives a perfect opportunity for students to identify different viewpoints about this news story. Another important element about viewpoints is shown in this lesson: A person who has a viewpoint on a news story has likely been affected by some element of that news. That impact may be somewhat abstract. In this news story, the impacts are direct and easier for our students to identify as they develop this element of their news literacy. This lesson uses a variation of Project Zero's Circle of Viewpoints activity.

Objectives

In this lesson, students will:

- View a televised news report to gain an understanding of a news topic.
- Identify individuals who are affected by that news topic.
- Predict, based on identified groups and given information, the viewpoint of an identified individual.

A Historic Perspective

Introduce the Lesson

Begin the lesson by asking students to identify something they care deeply about that someone in their family does not. This does not have to be news related. After a few students have had the opportunity to share, ask whether there are ever times when it is important to know that others may feel differently than you. Take any ideas from students.

Share with students the importance of understanding your own opinion on a news topic. Remind them that it is equally important to have an understanding that not everyone feels the same way you do about that same topic. Tell students that they are going to explore that idea through a news story on the 1979 gasoline shortages.

Begin the Activity

While distributing the organizer, share with students that they will watch the news story three times. During the first watch, students will view it through a lens of understanding the topic of the gasoline shortage at that moment: May 18, 1979. Ask students to document their understanding in the organizer, either by quoting passages from the news report or interviews, summarizing elements of the story in their own words, or both. After students have watched the news story, ask a few students to share their general understanding as a formative check before moving on. Although students will not have a complete grasp of the concepts around the event, they should be able to share general knowledge supplied by the report.

Next, make students aware that they may not have a viewpoint about this story, as they were not directly affected by it. Remind them that others were, though, and many of those people were either featured or referred to in the news story. For their second viewing, challenge students to find as many different viewpoints as they can. Define these as individuals, groups, organizations, or companies that are affected by the information presented in the story. If an example is needed, share one or both of these viewpoints:

- Traveling salesman
- Gas station (as a business)

Allow students to watch the news report a second time. When finished, have students share examples. If time allows, collect all student-identified viewpoints.

Move to the final viewing by inviting students now to predict how the individuals or groups with the different viewpoints they identified feel about the news topic. Share with students that some people in the news report may directly voice how they feel about the gas shortage. In other cases, students will have to make an educated guess based on what they know about the news topic and the viewpoint. If an example was used previously, return to it.

- Traveling salesman: Does not like the increased gas prices he must pay to do his job.
- Gas station (as a business): Appears to be making more money because of increased prices but must pay more for the gas it sells. The business is constantly dealing with unhappy customers.

As students prepare to watch the news story for the third time, invite them to select a viewpoint that someone else identified. After students watch the news report for the third time, ask students to share the perspective of some of their viewpoints. Take a moment to share multiple perspectives from the same viewpoint.

Discussion and Ending the Activity

Discuss:

- Why might we not always agree about what a person or group might think?
- How might individuals within a group be different? For example, why might all salesmen not agree on the gas shortage?

End the lesson with the exit slip.

A Modern Perspective

If students have some connection to a current news topic, they may also have a viewpoint on a related news story. Consider using a news story that most students would have a connection with. Local news stories may be of particular interest to students.

In this instance, students may self-identify as having a viewpoint. Prior to students revealing their own viewpoint, allow students to predict what some other viewpoints about the news topic may be, although they should not go so far as to try to identify any individual's viewpoint at this time.

As students reveal their own viewpoints to the class, individual students can reflect on what viewpoints they did not anticipate and which they did. This personal activity may also create an opportunity for overlapping viewpoints to be highlighted, when students may have similar viewpoints on a news topic but differ in a small but meaningful way.

Be considerate. Some news stories may elicit stronger emotional reactions if students have a personal connection to the topic. Remind students that a goal of the lesson is to identify viewpoints, not to judge or try to change them.

Differentiation

There are several moments of visual math that can be extended upon from this news story. Identifying gallons and price will give students data that will allow them to determine the price per gallon of gas at these stations when the footage was taken. Although additional sources will have to be found, students can also identify cars in the video footage, approximate the year the car was made, and find information on fuel capacity and fuel economy to determine the cost to fill the tank with gas, as well as how many miles the car would be able to travel on that tank of gas.

When sharing the perspective of one of the identified viewpoints, students might find it more impactful to speak as that individual or as someone from that group. Invite students to speak in first person when sharing these perspectives. Acknowledge, before students begin, that speaking in the first person to express what we believe is another's viewpoint may be does not necessarily mean that we agree with that viewpoint.

Assessment

Exit Slip	
What could be possible benefits to understanding a friend's or relative's viewpoint of a news story if that viewpoint differs from your own?	

REFERENCES

"Ch 17 Reports." WNED, American Archive of Public Broadcasting (WGBH and the Library of Congress), Boston, MA and Washington, DC. 18 May 1979. https://americanarchive.org/catalog/cpb-aacip-81-558czh4x?start=22.03 &end=383.87

"Circle of Viewpoints." *Circle of Viewpoints | Project Zero*, www.pz.harvard.edu /resources/circle-of-viewpoints

Organizer

News Event:
Source:

First Viewing: What is your understanding of the news event?	
Second Viewing: Who are individuals or groups that were affected by the news event, according to this news report?	Third Viewing: What do you think these groups' or individuals' viewpoints were about the news event?

References

Kavanagh, Jennifer, William Marcellino, Jonathan S. Blake, Shawn Smith, Steven Davenport, and Mahlet G. Tebeka. "News in a Digital Age: Comparing the Presentation of Information over Time and Across Platforms." RAND Corporation, May 13, 2019. https://www.rand.org/pubs/research_reports/RR2960.html.

"New Survey Reveals Teens Get Their News from Social Media and YouTube." PR Newswire, August 13, 2019. https://www.prnewswire.com/news-releases/new-survey-reveals-teens-get-their-news-from-social-media-and-youtube-300900557.html.

Robb, Michael B. "News and America's Kids: How Young People Perceive and Are Impacted by the News." *Common Sense Media.* www.commonsensemedia.org/sites/default/files/uploads/research/2017_commonsense_newsandamericaskids.pdf.

"Stanford History Education Group." *Stanford History Education Group,* n.d. sheg.stanford.edu.

Waldman, Loretta. "Schools Key to Solving Fake News Problem, Says UConn Expert." UConn Today, February 19, 2018. https://today.uconn.edu/2016/12/schools-key-to-solving-fake-news-problem-says-uconn-expert.

Waldman, Steven. "The Information Needs of Communities: The Changing Media Landscape in a Broadband Age." *Federal Communications Commission,* July 2011. transition.fcc.gov/osp/inc-report/The_Information_Needs_of_Communities.pdf.

"What Is News Literacy?" Center for News Literacy. https://www.centerfornewsliteracy.org/what-is-news-literacy.

Wineburg, S. (2018). *Why Learn History (When It's Already on Your Phone).* Chicago, IL: University of Chicago Press.

About the Author

TOM BOBER is a school librarian at RM Captain Elementary, 2018 *Library Journal* Mover and Shaker, former Teacher in Residence at the Library of Congress, and author of the book *Elementary Educator's Guide to Primary Sources: Strategies for Teaching* (Libraries Unlimited, 2018). He is a DPLA Community Rep, and a member of teacher advisory boards for the American Archive of Public Broadcasting and the National Portrait Gallery. Tom writes the Picture Books and Primary Sources posts for AASL's Knowledge Quest blog and is host of The Primary Source Podcast. He has written articles about students learning through the use of primary sources for several publications including *SLJ* (*School Library Journal*). Tom also presents at conferences, runs workshops, and gives webinars to promote the use of primary sources in student learning. His foundation is built on more than 20 years in public education as an elementary classroom teacher, educational technologist, and more than 10 years as a school librarian.

CPSIA information can be obtained
at www.ICGtesting.com
Printed in the USA
BVHW010215180721
612091BV00022B/140